Architects Draw

Architects Draw

SUE FERGUSON GUSSOW

Introduction by Dore Ashton

Princeton Architectural Press, New York

Architecture Briefs
The Architecture Briefs series takes on a variety of single topics of interest to architecture students and young professionals. Field-specific and technical information, ranging from hand-drawn to digital methods, are presented in a user-friendly manner alongside basics of architectural thought, design, and construction. The series familiarizes readers with the concepts and skills necessary to successfully translate ideas into built form.

Published by
Princeton Architectural Press
37 East Seventh Street
New York, New York 10003

For a free catalog of books, call 1.800.722.6657.
Visit our website at www.papress.com.

Editor: Linda Lee
Series Editor: Clare Jacobson
Production Editor: Steven Hillyer
Designer: Abigail Sturges

Special thanks to: Nettie Aljian, Sara Bader, Dorothy Ball, Nicola Bednarek, Janet Behning, Becca Casbon, Penny (Yuen Pik) Chu, Russell Fernandez, Pete Fitzpatrick, Wendy Fuller, Jan Haux, Aileen Kwun, Nancy Eklund Later, Laurie Manfra, Katharine Myers, Lauren Nelson Packard, Jennifer Thompson, Arnoud Verhaeghe, Paul Wagner, Joseph Weston, and Deb Wood of Princeton Architectural Press —Kevin C. Lippert, publisher

Library of Congress Cataloging-in-Publication Data
Gussow, Sue Ferguson.
  Architects draw / Sue Ferguson Gussow ; introduction by Dore Ashton.
    p. cm. — (Architecture briefs)
  Includes bibliographical references and index.
  ISBN-13: 978-1-56898-740-8 (pbk. : alk. paper)
  1. Architectural drawing—Technique. 2. Drawing—Technique. I. Title.
  NA2708.G87 2008
  720.28'4—dc22
                                      2007032649

Image Credits
Unless otherwise noted below, all illustrations in this publication have been reproduced courtesy of The Irwin S. Chanin School of Architecture of The Cooper Union.

Several individuals participated in the documentation of student work in Chapters 1 and 2. They include Amber Chapin, Steven Hillyer, Olivia Valentine, and Elizabeth van der Heijden. Large-format photography was accomplished with the assistance of James Kendi, Pro Lab, and Modernage Custom Imaging Labs.

Christina Condak 75
François de Menil 163, 165 (figures 5 and 6)
François de Menil, photo by Paul Warchol 165 (figure 7)
Mark Epstein 140
Firat Erdim 166
Paul Henderson 164
James Hicks 167
Karen Bausman + Associates 172 (figure 21)
Karen Bausman + Associates, photo by Jack Pottle / Esto 161, 172 (figures 22 and 23)
Peter Lynch, photo by Tim Thayer 170 (figure 17)
Morris Sato Studio 168 (figure 12)
Morris Sato Studio, photo by Carson Zullinger 168 (figure 13)
Stephen Mullins 55
OBRA Architects 170–71 (figures 18–20)
Reiser + Umemoto 169

TO JOHN HEJDUK

CONTENTS

ACKNOWLEDGMENTS

The realization of this book owes a debt to the many individuals who played a signal role in its development. From my initial notions of a book to the publication that has emerged, countless of my students' drawings were culled through. The participation of many individuals and institutions was required.

The Graham Foundation and the Tides Foundation awarded generous grants. Anthony Vidler, dean of The Irwin S. Chanin School of Architecture of The Cooper Union, allowed access to the photography collection of the school's Architecture Archive.

For their generosity and guidance, thanks are due to John de Cuevas and Sue Lonoff de Cuevas, François and Susan de Menil, and Toshiko Mori. My colleague Dore Ashton has been a mentor throughout. I wish particularly to thank my dear friend John Hejduk, the late dean emeritus of The Irwin S. Chanin School of Architecture, for the inception of this book. Over the years he would say, "Sue, let's do a book," and to that end drawings would intermittently be saved. A quarter century has passed since he first made that statement, and some of the drawings now show the yellowing of years.

My thanks go especially to my colleague Steven Hillyer, director of The Cooper Union Architecture Archive and production editor of this book. His extensive talents, vision, clear-headedness, and devotion were a mainstay from start to finish. Gina Pollara, former associate director of the Archive, also provided significant support and expertise through a portion of the work.

Considerable skill and hours of devotion were given by the project's major assistants and former students, Yeon Wha Hong, Anne Romme, and Dan Webre. Also on board were Jesicka Alexander, Lis Cena, Deborah Ferrer, Kalle Lindgren, Alexander Wood, and Monical Shapiro, who holds the history of the School of Architecture in her mind.

It has been a great pleasure to work with Executive Editor Clare Jacobson and Editorial Director Jennifer Thompson of the Princeton Architectural Press in shaping the focus of this book. For her painstaking attention to detail and her thoughtful observations I especially thank editor Linda Lee.

I am grateful to my students themselves—more than a thousand over nearly four decades of teaching—for their countless drawings and the passion they developed for the art of drawing. The rich diversity of their work and their words in response to projects set forth in these pages has further taught me how to teach.

Finally I thank my husband, Donald Gerard, for his patience in reading every single word, for the clarity (and necessity) of his critique, his editorial acuity, and most of all his enduring support and belief in the value of this book.

THE FREE HAND

DORE ASHTON

The nature of the act of drawing has been discussed for centuries—an indication of how fundamental it is to human endeavor. During the Renaissance, a period of great architectural invention, it was often architects who fervently addressed the issue of drawing. And no wonder, since among the great architects—I think of Michelangelo—drawing and painting were the natural accompaniments to the creation of articulated spaces. Speculative geniuses such as Leonardo never ceased pondering the nature of drawing, often making casual remarks in his journals of striking import, as when he characterized the contour line as possessing *uno spessore invisible*, "an invisible thickness."

Old rumors have it that Nicolas Poussin said there were two ways of regarding: the first is merely to look and the second is to look with attention. Poussin was seconded by Goethe, whose remarks on drawing occur from his earliest success in the novels, *The Sorrows of Young Werther* (1774), to his enigmatic *Elective Affinities* (1809); in the latter he particularly reveals his proclivity for landscape architecture. That text is peppered with remarks about the importance of art and drawing in the architect's life. Drawings give, in their purity, the mental attention of the artist, and they bring immediately before us the mood of his mind at the moment of creation.[1] In speaking of the mood of the mind, Goethe reminds us of the mysterious fusion of eye, hand, and mind that we call drawing and assumes that drawing springs from the imagination, the only site for a mood of mind. It is a faculty indispensable for an architect.

A draftsman is not a mere technician if he avails himself of what has long been called *freehand drawing*—a term by which we condense ideas about the reciprocity of eye, hand, and mind. The very act of drawing, if freely engaged, is speculative to the highest degree. Just as there are no two hands alike, there are literally boundless possibilities in the hand of each when touching the vast blankness of a page. There are countless testimonies to the value of such explorations. I have always liked especially the words of the poet Paul Valéry, who, while still a schoolboy, had the good fortune to watch Edgar Degas drawing, and was a decent draftsman himself. Valéry observed:

> There is an immense difference between seeing a thing without a pencil in the hand and seeing it *while drawing* it. Even the object most familiar to our eyes becomes totally different if one applies oneself to drawing it: one perceives that one didn't really know it, one had never really *seen* it.[2]

Valéry added a dictum from Ingres that he had heard from Degas: "The pencil must have on the page the same delicacy as the fly who wanders on a pane of glass."[3] Needless to say, such delicacy, with all its fortuities, is essential to an architect. The principal value to him in freehand drawing lies in the act of disciplining the whole organism—his own, that is—in order to understand with every fiber in his body the true nature of space. What architect can forgo speculating on the nature of space? The revelations, while drawing freely, are legion. Visual artists, amongst whom I include architects and poets alike, live in an inescapable quest of some defining vision of space. I have found it pervasive in the oeuvre of the Mexican poet Octavio Paz, who, in writing of the sculptor Chillida (who spent four years in architecture school), mused about space. He said it is "anterior to the I": "The apprehension of space is instinctive, a corporeal experience: before thinking it or defining it, we feel it. Space is not outside of us or a mere extension: it is that in which we are. Space is a *where*."[4]

Above all other artists, architects require a firm sense of where. They must first locate themselves and then their composed objects in an ideal space before they can even begin the sequence of acts that constitute a construction.

Poets, artists, and architects inevitably seek the metaphorical dimension of space. It was one of the primary means of instruction in the years that John Hejduk developed the curriculum at The Cooper Union. Metaphor, as Aristotle thought, is "a kind of enigma" and, for a verbal artist, "the greatest thing by far is to have a command of metaphor because this alone cannot be imparted by another; it is the mark of genius, for to make a good metaphor implies an eye for 'resemblances.'"[5] The eye, Hejduk thought, must be cultivated for myriad resemblances in the Aristotelian sense—that is, through a poetic exploration of both inner and outer spaces. Probably The Cooper Union was the only school in the world that had thesis projects with such titles as "A Blue House for Mallarmé" or "The City of Fools."

Hejduk was not alone among modern architects honoring the imaginative extensions of metaphor. One has only to read Louis Kahn's paeans to drawing scattered poetically throughout his writings to know how important his metaphorical sketches were to his architectural practice. There is a great difference, he knew, between drawing and rendering, and that difference made all the difference.

If we look at the sketchbooks of the renowned architects of the twentieth century—Le Corbusier, Frank Lloyd Wright, Kahn, and a host of others—we see immediately why the eighteenth-century French critics called the sketch a *premiere pensée*, "the initial thought." It would be the indispensable germ of the product we call architecture.

Hejduk's ideas about the training of the architect found a perfect executrix in Sue Gussow. Her knowledge as a practicing artist extended far back in history. She taught her students the freedom to range everywhere in time and space—that is, in the history of artists from cavemen on—in order to understand the vast range of modes of expression. Architects were trained to attend to the myriad methods artists have found to express what Goethe called the mood of their minds, without inhibitions. She accustomed these future professionals to the quest for the unaccountable, the mystery in establishing a metaphor for lived experience. She gave them, in short, a free hand.

PART I

DRAWING FROM LIFE
THE FUNDAMENTALS

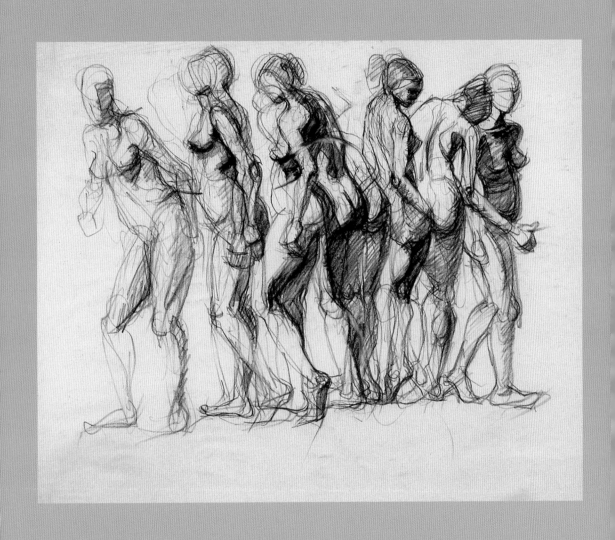

In the spring of 1975, I met with John Hejduk, the late dean of the Irwin S. Chanin School of Architecture of The Cooper Union, to discuss the possibility of my teaching a section of a class designated Freehand Drawing. A course by that title already in the curriculum was in need of reshaping. Hejduk wished to envigorate the design curriculum with a more liberating drawing program. "I want someone who can teach the figure," he declared to his close collaborator and colleague, the painter Robert Slutzky. Familiar with my studio work and my teaching in the School of Art, Slutzky arranged the appointment. The dialogue with Hejduk, begun in that meeting, continued for the next quarter century. Those conversations altered and enlarged the drawing curriculum. They illuminated and expanded my understanding of both drawing and teaching over the next three decades.

One might ask, why teach architects to draw from the figure at all? Wouldn't the logical program consist of plan, section, elevation, and perhaps perspective and axonometric drawing? Why not devise a course simply and expansively titled Drawing that would encompass all of the above and also embrace computer-generated drawing? What might an architecture student gain from a year-long intensive drill in drawing from observation—in drawing from life? The answer emanates from the body itself. So much of what the human creature has come to know has been learned from the body—from how it walks, rests, runs, and dances. Invert the phrase "Body of Knowledge" and it becomes "Knowledge of (the) Body."

The very concept of measurement begins with the parts and proportions of human anatomy—a foot, an arm's length, the distance of so many heads or hands. The notion of counting in tens derives from our fingers, our toes. The anatomical word for finger—*digit*—is also the term for each of the ten units in Arabic enumeration. The cubit, the length from the elbow to the end tip of the middle finger, is famously utilized in Genesis 6:15: God instructs Noah to construct his ark of gopher wood, three hundred cubits in length, fifty cubits in breadth, thirty cubits in height—the first known set of architectural specifications.

From the human skeleton stems primary notions of structure, of shelter and containment: the spine can be taken as a metaphor for uprightness; the rib cage embraces and protects our breath and heartbeat; the pelvis is a bowl for bowels, organs, and fetuses; and the skull frames our vision and houses

our very thoughts and imaginings. Our joints not only permit the complexity of our locomotion but anticipate the coming of the hinge and all the myriad inventions of joinery and architectural articulation.

But perhaps the most compelling reason to teach drawing from the figure is the liberating joy of it. It is where all drawing begins. A child makes marks, blotches, scribbles, then hard- or soft-edged geometric shapes, stacks them one on another and names them: mother, father, house, me. It is the self revealed on paper—a declaration and a need.

Drawing entails another form of measurement. From the vast panorama of what the eye perceives, one needs to isolate, translate, and transcribe an image and proportion it to fit the two-dimensional confines of a finite sheet of paper. What width of mark is best to describe a six-foot body on a 36"-high tablet? What drawing medium best suits that scale; what kind of mark suits a 6" × 9" sketchbook? As the figure is scaled to the measure of the page, other questions of space—and the making and marking of space—begin to assert themselves. This is what Hejduk profoundly understood when he commissioned me (in tandem with Slutzky for the first two years) to redefine the first-year Freehand Drawing program.

WHERE IT ALL BEGINS: PEAS IN A POD

Early on, I tell my students that I promise not to teach them anything "useful." This, of course, grabs their attention; it is not what they expect. In architecture curricula drawing typically is viewed as utilitarian, a course adjunct to the design studio. In most schools drawing simply involves drafting techniques, nothing more. Only rarely is drawing regarded as expanding architectonic thought, as part of the thought process itself. Texts that link architecture and drawing together are generally how-to books. They deal with plan, section, elevation—or they set forth specific modes of illustration, such as perspective—but they do not address the experience of space or depth.

In my approach to setting up foundational problems, I find it important to teach concept, technique, and skill but imperative to recognize and value divergence. I teach Freehand Drawing to empower rather than "instruct." Permeating through all the assignments and infusing all of the studio sessions is the concept of that metaphoric dimension—space. There is the obvious concept of space on the paper: it is blank or drawn upon. But how is one able to translate from the three-dimensional to the two-dimensional plane such factors as volume, transparency, and their interpenetration? The ability to master this is the underlying subtext of the course.

My first day of drawing class was a terrifying experience. Only seventeen, I had never contemplated an approach to drawing—much less thought about hanging any of my drawings on the wall and talking about them. Then there was Gussow, with this seemingly intimidating presence and a wide-brimmed hat to match. She was intensely serious about drawing. When it came to the first exercise, I practically carved the pea pod through the entire

pad of newsprint. The drawing was miniscule, in the middle of an enormous sheet of paper. But even by the second attempt to draw from an actual pea pod, I was already beginning to study what I was seeing much more carefully. That study, or searching of sight, grew over the course of the year and still lives with me twenty years later. — STEVEN HILLYER

The very first meeting of the Freehand Drawing class provides the opportunity to establish the philosophy of the course. Drawing always begins on that very day. For the first several years, I handled that day in various ways, but in 1979 I happened upon a paragraph in the "Talk of the Town" column in the *New Yorker*:

I was shelling peas from my garden the other afternoon, and the ancient figure (attributed to Rabelais) dropped into my mind: "As like as two peas in a pod." I let it drop on through. I would be disappointed if I found only two peas in a pod, and I would be surprised if they looked exactly alike. Some peas are square, some are hexagonal, some are cone-shaped, some are disc-like, some are even round, and in almost every pod there is one pea, squeezed into the middle or off at one end, that is one-tenth the size of the others. Nature—in my experience with apples and green beans and tomatoes and squash and carrots and red roses and robins and oak trees—is given to variety more than to duplication. One has only to observe, to open the mind as well as the eye, to pierce the generalization. Peas look alike as Chinese look to Westerners or Westerners to Chinese.[1]

On that very first day, the students are the proverbial peas in a pod. Their names appear on a printout—as yet unattached to faces. Although differentiated by gender, clothing, and other surface attributes, they all appear wonderfully—and similarly—young.

EXERCISES

Draw a pea pod from memory and in such a way that it reveals the peas it contains. Any drawing medium may be used, and any size paper will do. Approximately 30 minutes are allotted for one or several drawings. Students are assured that this is *not* a test and no instruction is given.

Then actual garden peas—in pods, of course—are distributed. The pod and peas are drawn once more—this time from observation. Another 30 minutes is allotted.

The *New Yorker* paragraph is read to the class and copies of it are distributed.

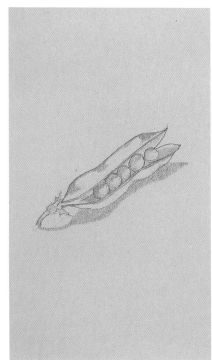

Figures 1, 2, and 3 (following page) are a classic set of pea-pod drawings. They clearly illustrate the issues of visual memory and observation and the evolution from generalization to the particular.

FIGURE 1

The canoe-shaped pea pod opens to reveal nearly identical spherical peas, somewhat graduated, like a string of pearls. The author's veining of the pod's semitranslucent walls and the notation of each wall's slim ledge reveal his particular memory of an actual pea pod. Through the use of a faint shadow, there is only a tenuous attempt to anchor the pod to the surface on which it sits.

FIGURE 2

The drawing testifies to the impact of actual observation: the pod now reflects how its burgeoning occupants have influenced its shape. The cast shadow securely hinges the pod to the flat plane it occupies. The way the slender piece of stalk attaches the pod to the vine is well observed. However, the peas still retain their generic (now same size) roundness.

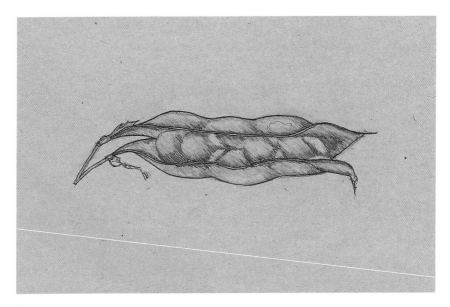

FIGURE 3

The pea pod ages. A small dried leaf is rendered in a spiraled curve. The vantage point is now from above—a more focused interior view. The peas are attached in an alternating pattern to either side of the pod's opening, knocking them out of the strict alignment seen in the earlier drawings. No longer entirely individuated, the peas cast shadows on each other; the shadow shapes move the eye along the pod's interior in a rhythmic fashion. The *negative space*—the leftover space between the peas—is delineated. The author has also created a mouthlike negative space at the split where the pod and stalk meet, echoing the open-mouth profile at the right created by the pod's curled-out, drying ends.

ASSIGNMENT

Reread the paragraph and draw the pea pods once more for next class meeting. Draw two other drawings: some aspect of the space in which each student presently lives and a self-portrait.

The pea-pod exercise forecasts the philosophy that will infuse the entire year-long program. Apart from the message implicit in the brief *New Yorker* passage, the absence of direct instruction on the first day suggests that the students will in many ways become their own teachers. Observation is a key player in the course and a faculty that must be honed.

Were it not for the capacity to generalize, it would not be possible to draw or even to think. But it is through disciplined observation that differentiation is clarified. The detail, the texture, the various shapes, the angle at which the light hits, the location of one's point of view are elements of study that lead a work from the generic to the specific and contain in them the magic of *visual surprise*. Surprise is the thing that caught your eye—the thing you did not expect to see. The question of what and how much to generalize, simplify, or edit out—and, conversely, what elements to emphasize, detail, and particularize—is crucial to the creative process. The balance struck between these two polarities must always be at the forefront of the critical discussion about the work.

CRITIQUE AND
THE DEVELOPMENT
OF JUDGMENT

During nearly four decades of teaching drawing at The Cooper Union, both in the School of Architecture and, until 1992, at the School of Art, I've had many occasions to visit other institutions. In art schools it is not typical to devote half the allotted class hours to critique. In schools of architecture, however, pin up and critique are more rigorously and frequently employed. In 1978, when I started to reframe the Freehand Drawing program, more frequent critique became the norm.

I believe drawing is best learned with the hand in motion, so initially I was reluctant to relinquish precious studio hours to critique. Yet drawing is thought extended through the fingertips. Strands of thought appear as marks on a field of paper: the eye perceives the embryonic image, the thinking/marking process takes place, the drawing emerges. Though I once believed that the act of making trumps debate, when teaching architects I discovered that the work progresses dramatically with frequent class critique—far beyond the rate at which it develops without it.

It is essential in a foundation program to devise assignments that are clear and that build upon and incorporate the concepts introduced in the preceding weeks. The assignment specifies the parameters, such as the subject, materials, number of drawings, and time allotted for each, and clarifies the portion of the assignment that is open-ended. Each assignment concludes with a *freestyle drawing*, in which the student has complete authority over material, size, or manner of drawing—that aspect commonly referred to as style.

At the beginning of each critique session, I ask the students what they discovered in executing the assignment, apart from achieving the implicit pedagogical goal. The pea-pod sequence is an introduction to careful observation. In the assignments that follow, students will investigate a variety of forms that illuminate concepts of drawing. These include the voluptuous, bodylike forms of bell peppers (see pp. 21–23), the curvilinear volumes that describe the human figure (see pp. 30–34), and the planar nature of paper bags (see pp. 62–65). These goals aside, the students always encounter unexpected ideas and epiphanies during the process. As the result of class discussion and student work, the assignments have evolved over the years. We learn from each other.

The judgment of the students is valuable from the beginning, although it must be honed and developed. At the weekly critique meetings, students select a favorite or compelling drawing from the walls—one that begs for discussion. It is with these drawings chosen by members of the class that the critical dialogue begins. The pedagogical goals in the assignment are recognized and internalized only as the work of each individual is presented and discussed. It is through their participation in these conversations that students begin to discover and develop their individual critical faculties. There is the given assignment, but there is also the assignment each student gives him/herself. There are no absolute rules or principles concerning drawing, only certain commonalities. It is these aspects of drawing that are valuable to explore.

Most projects continue for three to four weeks, and the drawings executed in subsequent weeks expand upon and incorporate the critique from the previous weeks. As the first-year course evolves, I introduce the layering of physical and psychological space. This complexity and randomness, in which "real" space is occupied by living beings, is the stuff of which art is made. This is what architecture shelters and celebrates.

BELL PEPPERS, GARLIC, BROKEN SHELLS, STILL LIFES

The pursuit of volume is of paramount intrigue in the art of drawing—the hand plotting out a web of lines to snare a three-dimensional form on a two-dimensional plane. The delight in seeing this fully rounded image emerge from the flat paper is equal only to the frustration and disappointment experienced when the drawing "falls flat." When volumetric illusion is achieved and the object drawn seems to rise from the paper, we pronounce it "true to life." Of course, it is not true at all. The paper remains forever flat. The form the drawing describes is an illusion; it is the magic of drawing that tricks the eye. Our purpose here is to learn magic tricks, to become magicians.

Concurrent with the first sessions of drawing from the live model, outside assignments are designed to expand the concepts of volume explored in life-drawing studio. When drawing the major masses of the body—head, chest, and hips—the first order of concern is their three-dimensional relationship around the central axis of the spine (see "Drawing from the Figure," pp. 30–34).

In the assignments that follow the bell peppers, garlic, and broken shells should be arranged in multiples and their rounded volumes considered in relation to one another. The concluding still-life project takes these volume/space concepts to a more complex realm.

FIGURE I

Bell Peppers

The fruit of the bell-pepper plant has long appealed to artists for its resemblance to the curves of the body's fleshed-out contours. The bell pepper possesses another significant dimension: apart from the undulations of its surface curves, it is a housing. In botany this fruit is termed an ovary—the primal housing. To the student of architecture, its function as a container and its interiority are as worthy of investigation and preoccupation as its outward voluptuous form.

The wall of this rounded globe of curved ribs develops around a pulpy mass in which the pepper's ovules or seeds are embedded. In the kitchen this pulpy mass is considered disposable waste, but it contains the botanic purpose of the plant. It is its future. The indentations delineating the curved ribs of the globe are an external expression of internal chambers, whose defining interior walls are formed by thin webs made of the same pulpy stuff as the central seed mass. As the pepper develops, these walls pull apart, and the chambers open, creating a vaulted hollow space. The pea pod's snug housing and the bell pepper's open chambers provide trenchant models for the organization of interior space.

It is critical early in the course to develop a dialogue between volume and void. Consider the object and the space it occupies; consider the space it contains—the void it houses and the manner in which this interior void opens (or does not open) to surrounding space. Also notice the object's spatial relation to the next object and the next—and the next. To achieve spatial magic in a drawing, all of this must be attended to—seemingly at once. To this end, the assignments usually call for multiples of the object to be drawn; this enforces the necessity of considering space in the design strategy.

ASSIGNMENT

Obtain two bell peppers. Leave one intact. Cut the other into two—or more—pieces, anywhere from two equal halves to any number of slices and proportions. Set the several pieces on a surface in a random arrangement, and draw them simultaneously as though there were an invisible spine connecting them. Freely use lines that wrap around the peppers' shapes. Do not draw only those lines that describe outside contours and rib indentations. Lines should also serve to indent the hollows and sculpt the bulging contours. As the eye travels back and forth from the whole pepper to the sliced portions, the hand should take account of the spaces between the pieces. Lines should describe, as well, the concavities of the segments' hollow interiors. For each of these five drawings, rearrange the peppers or change your vantage point. Set a strong single light source on the arrangement throughout the assignments. Draw five drawings with vine charcoal. 18" x 24" (or larger) newsprint pad. 5 to 10 minutes each.

Make a *blind-contour drawing* of at least two of the pepper pieces. In this method the eye slowly follows any line on the surface of the pepper—or its revealed interior—as the hand and pencil slowly record the eye's observation. In its classic form, a blind-contour drawing is made without the eye ever engaging the page. In the method we will employ here, the student may glance down rapidly—but infrequently—to judge the progress of a line. Drawing should then momentarily cease, starting again as the eye quickly resumes its focus on the line being studied. Scrutinize contours—i.e., outlines of shadows, highlights, details, and outer edges—equally. As progress should be painstaking and slow, consider the drawing finished—no matter how incomplete—in 1 hour. Freshly pointed pencil on 18" x 24" white paper.

Do a freestyle drawing. Any manner of drawing, provided the drawing is from observation and includes the pepper and pieces. Any drawing medium on any paper. 1 hour or more.

FIGURE 2

In this rapid study, a pepper is doubled over rather like a crouched human body—a challenging choice for a beginning student. The concavity of the bent forms is made emphatic by the gathered charcoal markings that follow the contours of each of the peppers' concavities and convexities. The missing lobe extracted from the pepper to the left remains a blank space and does not appear elsewhere on the page to give the pair a spatial reference. Here the intrigue with volume exists in its exterior expression.

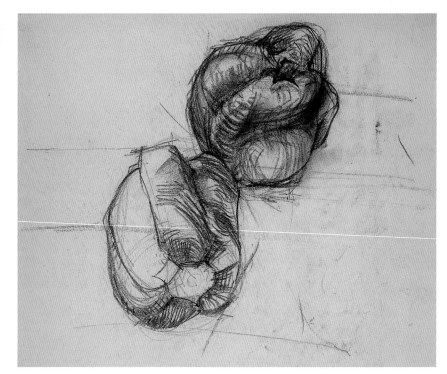

FIGURE 3

In this response to a blind-contour exercise, the author's eye has traveled along the edge of any observable shape making very little distinction between lighter or darker inflections of line—i.e., the shape of a highlight or shadow on the pepper's surface or the overlapping rings of shape created by the peppers' cast shadows are described with a similar surrounding edge.

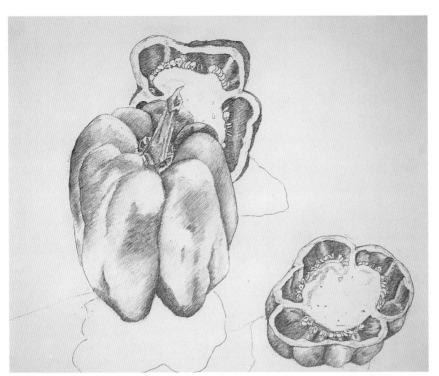

FIGURE 4

This freestyle study reveals the author's intense curiosity regarding the interior chambers of the sliced pepper. In true architectonic fashion, a section cut horizontally across the top quadrant of the pepper reveals the pulpy central mass with its embedded seeds. The drawing notes how pulpy walls emanate from this center to the exterior wall, defining the pepper's three chambers. The contrast between the satin gloss of the pepper's exterior surface and the texture of its bumpy interior are also carefully noted.

FIGURE 5

The left pepper in this freestyle rendition is cut along the indentations of its chamber walls. The leftmost piece, only partway severed, suggests that this segment is in the act of unfolding. This lends animation to the semicircular composition, held together by the contrasting statement of the plane of the table, whose topmost corner creates tension as it points toward the paper's edge. Charcoal *tone* is employed with eloquent gradation to indicate depth.

Garlic Bulbs

Garlic bulbs provide another opportunity to examine body-referent forms. Grouping and regrouping three or more bulbs (and a number of their separated cloves) creates a continuing space/design strategy. The structural arrangement of an individual garlic bulb is markedly different from the walled hollow of the bell pepper. Here, a compact mass of curved cloves is attached at bottom to a disc-shaped base from which a mop of roots descends. The compacted cloves are shaped snugly to one another around a very slender central core. The flesh of each clove is wrapped in its own skin; four or five translucent skins provide overall structural support, packaging the cloves in their wrapping. Each of these skins girdles the bulbs' gathered mass then twists about at the top, forming a stalk.

ASSIGNMENT

The assignment for drawing garlic bulbs follows the format given for the bell peppers. Leave two of the bulbs intact; extract several cloves of the third. Draw the three bulbs together with the separate cloves (virtually at once in the 5 to 10 minute drawings). Materials follow the same format given in the bell-pepper assignment.

FIGURE 6

Three complete garlic bulbs are each drawn with careful attention—the center and right bulbs in a linear mode derived from the blind-contour exercise. Several of the three garlics' thin skins appear to have been removed so that the burgeoning cloves might be explored in all their interdependent complexity. The presence of a remaining translucent wrapper is made evident by the elegantly drawn striations that follow the cloves' curves. The skin of the left garlic is the only area rendered in tone suggesting a deeper *local color* than the smooth unwrapped cloves on its left. (Local color is the surface color of an object—white, grey, black, red, green. In drawing, local color is translated to grayscale, to the tone it might appear in a black-and-white photograph.) The vertical center of the composition is just left of the right bulb's ascending twist of skins, and the greater bulk of the almost-symmetrical group is pushed to the left of the page and held in balance by the large negative space on the right.

FIGURE 7

The four bulbs are in varied postures, but in each the fascination rests equally between the mop of root mass and the intricate configuration of cloves. So much detail might prove distracting were it not for the *passageway* the dark shadow tone provides. (Passageway is a strategy for leading the viewer's eye through the drawing. It can be achieved by linking darker shapes or employing lines that continue from one object to another.) If one squints one will note there are three shapes of connected darker tones that join to one another. A secondary lighter gray describing *cast shadows* joins the bulbs into two major groups and also creates a hinge to the ground plane.

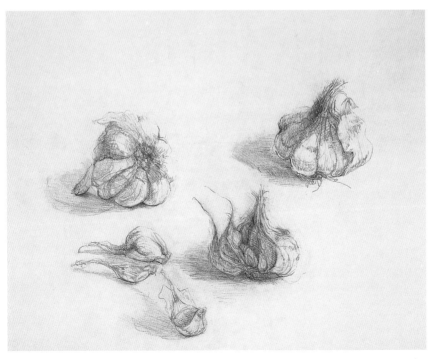

FIGURE 8

Each garlic bulb and separated cloves are presented in varying stages of deconstruction from whole to unwrapping to pulling apart. The story of this process animates the drawing in a zigzag gesture from top right downward to a lone foreground clove. Each step is superbly documented and sensitively drawn, but it is narrative rather than compositional structure that holds the drawing together. Note especially the garlic coming apart to reveal its many separated cloves—drawn as if the event of separating were generated from within the garlic itself.

Knobbed Whelk and Moon Snail Shells

Approximately one hundred miles east of The Cooper Union, the Long Island shores are punctuated with broken whelk and moon snail shells. (Entire shells are rare.) Unbroken shells in all their variety have long attracted human attention. Widely used as money, for jewelry, and as collectibles, their caverns and curves have delighted the eye and hand for millennia. For one who draws they offer an opportunity to examine the dialogue between volume and captured space. Rembrandt's haunting etching of a lone auger shell is a striking example of the undamaged shell's enchantment.[1]

However, it is the broken shell that will attract our attention here. Both their plenitude and their fractured condition make them worthy objects for an architecture student's drawing investigation. The seashell is at once armor and housing for its occupant, the mollusk. In a broken state the intricacy of the internal structure, and its former use, is revealed. In a majority of found shells, dashed by waves or attacked by gulls, both the concave walls and the convex inner chambers are simultaneously revealed. Certain shells, less frequently found, are ground down by sand over time to a spiraling inner core—a twisting spine just hinting at the walled chamber that once wrapped around it.

The term *spiral*, both a noun and a verb, embraces form and declares a continuous curvilinear motion. All shells in embryonic state are formed around a spiral.[2] In addition to the twisting counterpoint of inner core and outer chambers, the outer surfaces of the walls are themselves inscribed with the spiraling grooves of the shell's formation. The knobbed whelk shell's protuberant bumps punctuate yet another spiral formed by the shell's outer ledges. These features of the shell's formation seem to guide the hand as it draws.

FIGURE 10

The author of the drawing chose shells with minimum damage. The center whelk shell sports only the smallest round break—suggesting a spy window or peephole. It is the volume of the shells, their function as containers, that is of interest here, as the top right moon snail shell with its spiraling channel clearly indicates. Tonal gradations enhance the configuration of the shells (each positioned differently), enforce the shells' roundness, and create cast shadows that marry the shells together and distinctly define the ground plane.

FIGURE 11

The drawing declares the author's fascination with details, presented as minor structures supported by a major structure. The eponymous knobs that punctuate the whelk shell's outer ledges are clearly articulated, each with its particular and volumetric dimension and precise location on the spiraling ridge. A break in the wall of the largest shell provides a window on the curved and satin-surfaced interior.

Where portions of the shell have been broken away the edges are jagged, in contrast to the shell's swelling curves. This suggests that planar lines might be employed, together with the curving spiral, to capture the shell's spatial complexity.

ASSIGNMENT

The broken-shell assignment follows the format given for the bell-pepper and garlic drawings in all portions and all media. Use a minimum of three to five broken shells, and draw them together simultaneously.

Note: In the blind-contour portion of the assignment, draw quite slowly. Let the eye and hand travel from one shell to another, neither hurrying the investigation nor being concerned with the completion of the drawing.

Still Lifes

At the start of the 1993–94 academic year, John Hejduk commissioned all of the five design studios to explore the same problem: the design of a house. In fifth year, the thesis class was given the topic of still life as an avenue into "the house." As a response, a still-life project was assigned in Freehand Drawing to encourage dialogue between the first-year and thesis classes. In preparation the first-year class studied many of the great still-life painters—notably Jean-Baptiste-Siméon Chardin, Paul Cézanne, Georges Braque, and Giorgio Morandi. The two following examples of student work did not chronologically follow the pepper and garlic assignments—although they fit here schematically. They were completed later in the semester when concepts of passageway, density, transparency, and space had been explored.

Figure 12

Transparency and overlap are the most striking features. In exploring the relative location of various items—the bottle, the crate, pepper segments, etc.—they were drawn and then redrawn, their overlap lending the work both transparency and animation. The dense center arena of the drawing has an implicit grid structure suggested by the actual grid configuration of the crate. As the eye follows darkened linear paths through the jumble of fabric, fruit, and containers, a cityscape comes to mind.

FIGURE 13

Landscape serves as a metaphor here, while the strong vertical of the bottle at the top suggests a tower. Linear pathways lead from the rounded fruit and vegetables to the surrounding tousle of fabric in which they are nestled. The round forms, the area of gray *hatching* suggesting a valley, and the light nuanced handwriting of the surrounding fabric all speak of a more open environment than figure 12 proposes.

FIGURE 1

DRAWING FROM THE FIGURE

In the first year of my education at The Cooper Union, I drew every week from live models. I loved doing that. It was sometimes a physically draining experience, having to stand for hours, but a luxury nonetheless, to be able to scrutinize the body's form. The moving-figure exercise is basically observing the body in its actual physical space and translating that into the space of the page.

That we were constantly reminded to think of the space of the page is very important— it is the first critical act, how to place a mark on the page. Because you cannot plan out the composition of a drawing with this exercise, you become aware of how each decision affects the entire drawing and that there are also many more opportunities to change the entire movement of the composition and invent how the figures relate to each other on the page.

I became a lot freer about how I used the page with the moving-figure exercise. I could leave large areas untouched to concentrate on a single shift of the structure of the model's stance or fill a page with figures in a space. This exercise evolved into my advanced drawing work over the next few years of my education. — YEON WHA HONG

Learning to draw from the figure is not unlike learning to play a musical instrument or learning to dance. It requires constant and routine practice until it becomes part of the body's own language. A kinetic empathy develops. One's own anatomy begins to echo the thrust of the model's pelvis, the weight of the head bent forward, the strain of the neck, the pressure of the sole of the foot against the flat plane of the floor. Over time the body of the model on the platform imparts the way it must be drawn; the drawing seemingly draws itself.

After several weeks, once a reasonable proficiency in describing volume and gesture and scaling the entire figure to fit the page is gathered, drawing from the skeleton itself begins. This takes place parallel to the outside assignments of drawing monkeys, their skeletons, and dinosaur skeleton drawings (pp. 43–54).

EXERCISES

WEEKS I–III

In the first working session with a live model, there will be only short five-minute poses. Most of the students have never drawn from a nude model before, and in the case of some few who have, it is only rarely with instruction.

Using large newsprint pads, scale the entire figure—from head to foot—to the paper. Consider the major masses of the body, how they are capable of contrapostal twist upon the central axis of the spine, and emphasize this rotation of masses—more commonly referred to as *gesture*. The poses should all be standing. The anguish and challenge of *foreshortening* demanded by a reclining or seated nude will be introduced a few weeks later.

Consider the gestalt of the figure—draw it all at once. Use soft vine charcoal, a very forgiving, albeit messy, material that can cover a lot of territory rapidly. It is a humble medium requiring only the rub of the palm or fingers for erasure. It is also a medium that does not make the work look better than it deserves.

WEEKS IV–VI

By now students are generally capable of coping with the objectives outlined above. Two models are booked for the studio sessions, each one posing for approximately thirty minutes until the other steps onto the model stand (later they pose in pairs). This allows for a gathering of drawing momentum, which would otherwise be interrupted by the model's periodic rest breaks. Later, the models are posed in longer and increasingly complex compositions—initially of an hour's duration and then 2 to 3 hours. Objects, mirrors, and furniture are introduced during longer poses.

During the following weeks, draw the live models at an increasingly rapid pace. Stage Figure in Motion poses in which each posture the model takes changes incrementally from the previous one, as in stop-motion photography. Poses are now 1 to 2 minutes. Track the figures across the page. Add crouched and reclining poses. Introduce foreshortening.

FIGURE 2

The author staged a highly choreographed event out of the dense overlay of the model's poses. The arm of the figure sitting at bottom right gestures upward. The drawing heralds a progressive rising movement from crouching to fully standing and rotating postures. Around the darkened core of overlaid marks at the left of center, the drawing flares out and circulates, much as the standing figures appear to circulate around the lower tier of crouched bodies. The whole of the drawing assumes a gesture that is greater than any individual pose.

FIGURE 3

The model's poses are positioned to enhance the illusion of the page as a theatrical setting. A figure scaled to be taller than the vertical dimension of the page exits through the left foreground corner, and his scale creates a middle ground, a stage on which bodies in profile lunge in diametric opposition. Their athletic strides create a compelling negative V shape to the right of center, forcing the figures to the right out of the arena of the page. The bold, geometric use of negative areas—enhanced with dark hatching—make this a drawing in which narrative and design meet to mutual advantage.

FIGURE 4

It is the gesture of marking that activates the page. The model continues to be a presence; however, the posture of the body, lightly rubbed in, is a transparent memory of a previous pose. Note bold overriding calligraphy of colored-oil-bar marks that occasionally breaks loose from describing individual figures and dances on its own.

Incremental stopped motion is the subject of figures 5 and 6.

FIGURE 5

The drawing tracks the model from the left to the right of the page. Standing with a casual arms-folded posture, the figure gathers momentum and descends at midpage to a series of crouched postures. Progressing on hands and knees, he begins to rise up again at the right. The standing and crouched poses are framed in two essentially rectangular blocks with a responding square-shaped void in the upper right quadrant of the page. The crouching sequence with its dense overlap resembles a spine in its incremental movement and subtle upward curvature.

FIGURE 6

The model seems to rotate in the dance of arm-linked women. The rotating positions of heads and the crossed-over posture of legs imply a central spatial-core pivot. Some barely drawn limbs trace movement too rapid to record, while the density of marking of the central figure(s) underscores the notion of a core. The women circle at the right of the page as a large block of negative space at the left suggests an arena into which the group might next rotate.

FIGURE 7

This work presents an array of stages through which a drawing might evolve. From transparency to density, from tentative and unfinished to volumetric and fully realized, from smudged and erased to confident handwriting, the work celebrates the pleasure (and the frustration) of drawing. By drawing postures that range from rising up from the ground to emphatic undulating poses, the student has choreographed an exuberant dance.

THE FIGURE IN A CHAIR

A day in drawing class is like the Big Bang backward: we move toward center. The model is a distant, frustratingly capricious speck at first. Students form a wide, tightening loop of easel legs and hands and eyes. The shoulder of one bumps the drawing board of another with the occasional clatter and dropped chalk. We become something akin to the multicolored rings of planets or belts of spiraling stones. As we get closer to the model, her movements slow until she is finally, monumentally still.

A seated figure, the model is no longer a body seen in the round. She is the press of an arm against a chair's curve, the weight of a thigh upon folds of cloth. Though she sits motionless, she—as all celestial centers—has a latent movement that we discover as we draw. She extends impossibly off the page, needing to be drawn larger than we initially imagine. The class, we realize, is not cosmically inverted after all. We scatter at the end of the day, leaving our circle of easels in the empty room.

— AMBER CHAPIN

From Rietveld to Le Corbusier to Eames to Gehry to Hejduk, noted modern architects have famously designed chairs. In the cases of Gaudí, Macintosh, and Wright, it is inconceivable to imagine their architecture furnished by another's designs. From throne rooms to lecture halls to parlors to barber shops, chairs have assumed a variety of forms. In a broad array of cultures and eras, chairs have reflected the aesthetic aims of the architecture that houses them.

The body, in a standing posture, distributes its weight through the lower limbs to the ground plane. In a recumbent position, weight is distributed downward through those portions of the body that touch the plane upon which it reclines. The chair is a human mediation between the standing and the supine figure. Depending on the structure of the chair and the posture of its occupant, weight is distributed in various and complex ways. It is common that many architectural careers at some point encompass furniture and chair design. For the student of architecture the chair and its occupant possess a special significance as subject matter for drawing.

To take a load off your feet—as the phrase goes—and place that load on the plane of a chair's seat redistributes the weight of the mass of the torso, head, and arms to the chair's structure. The seated figure then becomes a six legged, two- or four-armed creature. (Of course, different arithmetic applies to the three-legged stool and the pedestal chair.)

Thought of in this light, the newly conceived chair/person must be drawn all together—at least in the initial stages of the work. The common beginners' strategies—drawing the person and then adding lines for the chair—or a more sophisticated approach—drawing the chair first and then inscribing the body within its framing—each are ill-fated tactics. In either case the figure

FIGURE I

and chair are destined for malproportion and a lack of the illusion of gravity. When drawing the figure seated in a chair, bear in mind that each takes the measure of the other. Drawing the two together at once implies understanding them as an interdependent system.

EXERCISES

Begin sessions with rapid drawings of the figure in a chair. (Chairs that are fairly open—with fretted backs or other see-through attributes—are best for the beginning of this exercise.) Move the model and chair in a snaking path along the studio floor at ten- to fifteen-minute intervals. Change the pose incrementally—the model might raise or lower the head, move a hand from chair arm to knee, slide a foot further out along the floor. Request that the model make only one change per posture, not several. Overlap poses on the same sheet to chart the figure/chair's progress along the floor. Vine charcoal. 24" x 36" newsprint or large sheets of brown kraft paper. 30 minutes to 1 hour.

Long studies of 2 to 2½ hour duration follow.

Over a few subsequent weeks, attempt the following variations:

Close-up View/High Vantage Point. Make a tight ring around the model, as close as the number of students and expanse of the easel bases will permit. (If two models are engaged, the class may be divided in half so that the two circles can draw closer to the model.) The resulting high, close vantage point gives fresh insight to point of view. For instance, a hip may appear to emerge beneath a shoulder, an ear lobe might punctuate the shape of a thigh. The drawing eye is in for surprises, thus the drawing that results will provide a refreshing spatial variation on the standard view of the seated pose. (A low vantage point—the student seated close to the model on the floor—is another variation on this theme.)

Collaboration. Since an assessment of relationships between figure, chair, and negative space is crucial in effecting a solid-looking work, it is useful to build in a critique of how well the eye is measuring. After the initial 15 or 20 minutes of working from the pose, move to the easel on your right and continue to draw, now on your neighbor's drawing, reassessing the drawing's measurements. Check on the negative space and overall relationships—chair legs to human legs, arms, etc. Continue this remeasuring/redrawing for approximately 15 minutes. Then return to your own drawing and remeasure the previous person's critique of it. At first this may prove to be a frustrating exercise. (You feel reluctant to mark up your colleague's drawing, and your own drawing has just been attacked.) However, great gains are often made from this exercise, both in learning to remeasure and alter initial efforts and in increasing assertiveness. Once the drawing has been "corrected," its author is forced to make bolder marks to inscribe new intentions.

Double Figures (and Chairs) Placed in Close Proximity. This creates a tangle of chair and human legs. Negative space plays a key role in sorting out legs, rungs, and chair locations as well as in assessing the two-headed, multilimbed creature before you. It should be stressed that drawing everything all together is of critical importance.

Note: Any of the above studio assignments may be combined with one another—Collaboration with High Vantage Point or these two with Double Figure—or all three together.

Long studies of 2 to 2½ hour duration follow. Any mutable drawing medium may be used: vine charcoal, soft charcoal pencil, pastel, conté crayon. Attempt oil bar if the initial marks are light; follow with bolder assertive marks as the drawing progresses.

FIGURE 2

Several quick figure/chair studies are distributed across the page. The model's pose remains constant, but for each pose interval the chair is repositioned incrementally. In the top right study the chair is only slightly noted, and the figure almost appears to levitate. In the central studies, the deeper investigation of the figure/chair increases the illusion of gravity. Note also the weight of the model's head leaning against his supporting arm and the slump of his torso into the contours of the chair. The chair legs are as fully reported as the human legs, acknowledging their structural necessity.

FIGURE 3

The drawing reveals evidence of remeasurement in the markings along the model's back and at her foreground knee. These markings, together with reworked dark areas (sometimes not coinciding with the figure/chair's contours), lend a boldness and vibration to the work. The student stood close to the model, and the high vantage point serves to pivot the two heads outward in front of the picture plane. The pivot point of the combined figures is at the toe of the foreground shoe. A web of lines in the background locates the legs of easels and a drawing pad, tilting the perspective of the floor plane forward.

FIGURE 4 *facing page*

Two figures nest in close proximity in the center portion of the page. Furnishings and architectural notations contain the figures in physically and psychologically differentiated postures. The left foreground table top, supporting a cushion taken from a sofa, counters their central location. While not a structural device in reality, the cushion's cut-out curve and the shadow cast upon it echo and support the woman's hand, suspended loosely at the wrist from her outthrust arm. The man's darkened horizontal shoe supports and emphasizes his more upright posture.

FIGURE 5 *right*

The chair's understated wire legs contrast with the sitter's weighted posture, creating an intriguing tension. A vertical seam, starting at the bottom right edge of the model's left trouser leg jumps to the vertical edge of the chair back and is picked up again as a fabric fold just under the chin. This vertical cut counters the figure/chair's tilted thrust toward the left edge of the page. Given the inward focus of the model—eyes closed, intent on his own music—the off-kilter posture is psychologically accurate.

FIGURE 6 *left*

The drawing is a witty riff on legs and framing. The top edge of the frame cuts off the two figures at about elbow height. All that appears of the standing figure at left is one leg and a portion of arm and hand. That leg obscures and substitutes for a chair leg. Similarly, the right leg of the seated woman conceals a second chair leg. What is created is a four-legged creature, three of whose legs are human. Dark horizontal bands echo the composition's framing; the distant baseboard links up with the miniskirt across the model's lap, repeated again by vertical strips that represent the chair seat and rung. At the base the dark shadow shape mirrors the triangle created by the woman's legs, also echoed by the smaller triangle her high-heeled shoe creates meeting the floor.

FIGURE 1

The scribble exercise merges with the rapid figure drawings. Vigorous, looped lines propel the eye across the top portion of the page, and outstretched arms that windmill across the top portion of the page emphasize this activity. The squatting figure at bottom center, with arms akimbo, punctuates the wildly gesturing motion throughout the page.

HANDWRITING: THE SCRIBBLE PAGE

The Freehand Drawing course runs along two parallel tracks: the weekly studio sessions for drawing from the model make up one track. On the other track, the class also meets weekly for another session devoted to critique. Here both drawings done in studio and work from outside assignments are pinned up and discussed. As the semester proceeds, drawing concepts are introduced and layered into the weekly assignments, and drawing from the model begins to deepen the understanding of these concepts.

At approximately midsemester, the scribble page is introduced—the timing for this varies with the class's grasp of earlier goals. Until this point little emphasis has been given to the grace or authority of the hand. In fact, the class has been cautioned not to approach drawing with "artistry." Having lost some of their previous drawing conceits, the moment is ripe to present the handwriting/scribble page and to speed up the timing of the model's poses.

The amusing body of work the artist Saul Steinberg presented in his book *The Passport*

(1954) sparked the following exercises. In it he replicates passports, diplomas, governmental decrees, marriage licenses, and other documents, drawn in all manner of scriptlike writing, such as signatures with bravura flourishes, which, upon closer inspection, contain no real words or letters.[1]

EXERCISES

Rapidly fill a page with "scribble"—writing that is mimetic of the movement of the hand in script writing but with the avoidance of making clear letters or words. In the first week, vine charcoal on 18" x 24" (or larger) newsprint. Later, use any media. No more than 1 or 2 minutes.

Note: This is a good exercise for experimenting with new media.

Tour the room to observe each other's pages. Variety is a given. It is the same remarkable and infinite variety one encounters in handwriting, fingerprints, and snowflakes. Return to the drawing pads and wipe down the page with your palm, side

of hand, or fingers to soften but not to entirely erase the marks. Apply this erasure unevenly. Superimpose scribble handwriting once again on the same paper, this time varying density and considering line weight to create darker and lighter areas.

Scribble and partly erase another such page, and then move into rapid figure drawing (poses of anywhere from 30 seconds to 2 minutes), keeping the same energetic and fluid calligraphy of the hand achieved in the scribble pages.

The drawings that result from this exercise are seductively sophisticated, resembling variations of a Cy Twombly and hinting at any number of Abstract Expressionist painters. More importantly it is an enlivening exercise, a way to loosen up the hand. Thereafter, the class begins each studio session with this exercise.

FIGURE 4

The momentum of
scribbled handwriting moving into drawing takes a
more consciously designed
tack. While some bodies
emerge from the writ-
ing—notice the middle and
far-right figures scribbled
in red—other more visibly
pronounced bodies, in
black, border a strand
of writing suspended
between them on the
upper middle ground.

FIGURE 5

Handwriting itself is no longer seen, but the evidence
and energy derived from
the scribble exercise infuses
the process and rhythms
of the page. Figures are
rubbed down and redrawn;
ghosts of bodies and marks
that suggest disembodied
gestures continue to whis-
per on the page. The fig-
ures move across the paper
in two tiers, resembling
pictographic lines of text.

MONKEYS, SKELETONS, DINOSAUR BONES

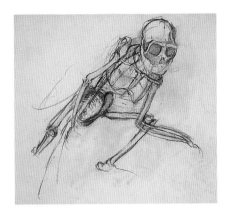

FIGURE I

The hand speaks to the brain as surely as the brain speaks to the hand. — ROBERTSON DAVIES, *What's Bred in the Bone*

Monkeys

Monkeys make first-rate models. Their groupings, their chatter, their articulate hands grooming and gesticulating all point out their uncanny resemblance to us. As monkeys scamper around, it is difficult to record their movements. The handwriting exercise is an ideal precursor to this exploration of drawing a volume in motion across a field of paper.

Coordinating with the Monkeys in Motion assignments at Central Park Zoo, the students are also asked to study monkey skeletons at the Museum of Natural History. At this same point in the semester, live models and human skeletons are being posed side-by-side in weekly studio sessions (see pp. 51–54).

ASSIGNMENT

Track the movements of the monkeys across the page. As the design evolves, observe their groupings and individual postures. At the same time, notice the spaces created between these clusters and the separate monkeys. Do not draw small, individuated monkey portraits; render the monkeys as they scuttle about. Consider how drawing this activity will provide a passageway or gesture to move the viewer's eye across the paper. Two or three pages— the first page in vine charcoal on 18" x 24" (or larger) newsprint, the following pages in any preferred drawing medium on any paper. About I hour.

Museum of Natural History. Draw the monkey skeletons from three different points of view, each time depicting the entire skeleton at once, seeking gesture and volume and avoiding a bone-by-bone description. Consider the skull, ribcage, and pelvis as containers of volume around the axis of the spine. Vine charcoal. 18" x 24" (or larger) newsprint. 10 to 15 minutes per drawing.

Blind-contour Drawing. Draw the contour or edges of the skeleton. Do not look down at the paper, save for occasional momentary glances. The pencil traces the slow movement of the eye across the skeleton, bone-by-bone, each edge described by a sharp, hard line. Do not erase. Let the drawing contain the history of the edges the eye traversed. The exercise should be accomplished with painstaking slowness, with a relatively hard, sharpened pencil or pen on white paper. 45 minutes to I hour.

Freestyle Study. Encompass all or most of the skeleton in an underdrawing. An underdrawing is a light, rapid study in which the artist marks the major masses and thrusts of the figure or object under consideration. It is kept light so that subsequent marks can further define the artist's gathering intention. Investigate some major aspect of the structure with a sharper focus, always with reference to its relation to the spine—ribcage to spine, limb to pelvis to spine, etc. Any medium or paper. At least I hour.

FIGURE 2

The drawing reveals true
hand-to-eye engagement.
There is clear evidence of
lighter underdrawing with
a second level of darker,
more emphatic marks
that assert the bending
of a spine, the flexing of
a haunch. The viewer's
gaze transverses the
page, guided by certain
implicit visual pathways.
For instance, the eye might
begin at lower left, ascend
vertically, and descend
in clockwise fashion. The
stone ledges on which
monkeys sit or clamber
are not drawn; they are
implied by the position
of the monkeys' rumps,
which form a series of
brief, broken horizontal
lines. Most important is
the evident engagement of
the student's hand, mind,
and eye—all in constant
conversation.

FIGURE 3

The stop-motion account
of an individual monkey's
activity loops its progress
from seated to walking to
seated once again. Rapid
underdrawing of major
masses is evident as the
student envisions the
skeleton and the body's
major masses beneath the
fur. The darker marking
builds the form and further
animates the gesture of
each posture.

FIGURE 4

The animation of the drawing attests both to its author's fluid hand and to the compelling drama of the skeleton's posture. Observe the assertive range of calligraphic writing that descends in a spiral from the skull, through the ribcage, pelvis, knee, and eventually to the paw. Confidently placed shapes of tone create a handsome counterpoint to the elegant line.

Figures 5 and 6 are by the same student and attest to drawing as a process in which more than one study is made toward a final outcome.

FIGURE 5

The fluidity of line in the drawing, a deftly drawn precursor to figure 6, enhances the monkey skeleton's staged animation.

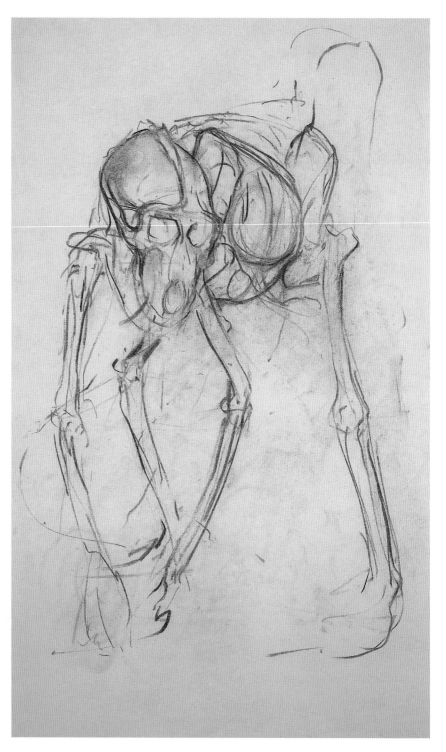

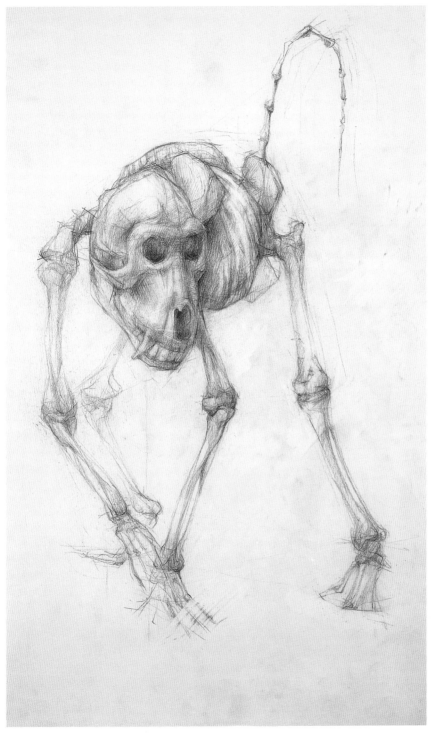

FIGURE 6

The drawing is a testament to both the author's masterful craft and acute observation. The dark creates a passageway across the drawing, moving in small staccato increments along the arched tail. After punctuating intervals in the rib cage, the dark tone moves on to become an uncanny black gaze, then descends along the creature's left fore and hind paws. The issue of focus also comes into play. The more darkly incised left hind foot is brought forward to the same plane as the left hand, enhancing the spine's motion forward. The almost head-on point of view furthers the illusion of the skull's being thrust in front of the picture plane.

Dinosaurs

After a couple of weeks of drawing monkeys and their bones, the next project is to draw from the museum's dinosaur skeletons. Here, issues of scale and structure are dramatically evident. The sequence of assignments here essentially follows that of the monkey skeleton sequence.

ASSIGNMENT

Draw the entire dinosaur skeleton. The challenge here is to scale such an enormous form to the size of the page. These are relatively quick studies, each drawing taking 15 to 20 minutes. Again, draw the three studies from different vantage points, avoiding the most conventional view, the profile. Vine Charcoal. 24" x 36" (or larger) newsprint.

Blind-contour Drawing. Reinterpret the blind-contour as a negative-space drawing, with the following difference: the contour lines define the spatial intervals between bone and bone. This time, the focus is on the negative or leftover space, not the bones. Pointed pencil or pen on white paper. In 1 hour consider the work finished.

Freestyle Study. Draw a part of the entire skeleton. Reference an adjoining skeletal structure—for example, ribcage to spine to beginning of pelvis, skull to neck to beginning of ribcage, or limb to pelvis to spine. Next, make a freestyle drawing where an underdrawing of the entire skeleton is the first step. As with the monkey assignment, bring a portion of the skeleton into greater focus upon this scaffolding. Any medium on any paper. 1 hour each drawing.

Figure 7

Flat patterning results from the negative-space/blind-contour approach. Due to the fact that it is not a profile perspective, the drawing achieves an intriguing and unexpected pattern. Careful observation, of the talons in particular, has lent the drawing an element of charged surprise. The way the drawing is framed also contributes to its success. The creature, all but contained by the page, with a small portion of the spine sliced off by the top edge of the paper, appears to be entering the space of the page from above, the talons of its forelimbs moving menacingly toward the viewer.

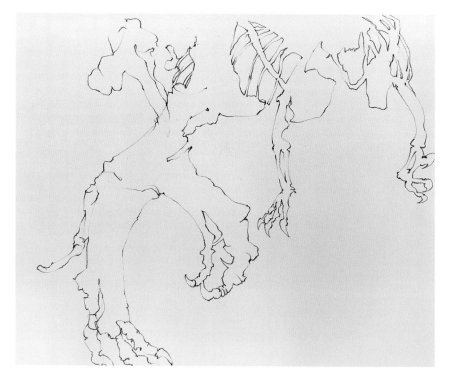

FIGURE 8 *right*

The drawing successfully addresses two difficult drawing challenges: scaling the immense skeleton to a 36" x 24" sheet of paper and the foreshortening resulting from this all-but-frontal vantage point, which made it necessary for the author to choose a perspective from beneath and through the ribcage and to observe the neck and skull from underneath. Momentum gathers in an abrupt curve starting at the open-jawed skull and moves along the spine, which diminishes in scale and focus into the illusory distance. In the underdrawing's tracery of light marking, changes in measurement are noted. The drawing's darker, more focused lines bring the forepaws, neck, and skull dramatically forward.

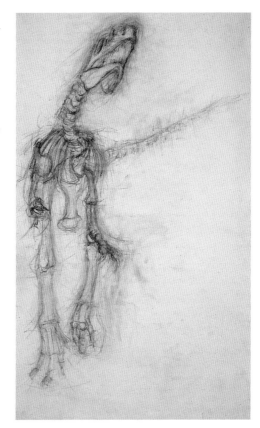

FIGURE 9 *below left*

A number of essential drawing strategies are illustrated. The work states a hierarchy of parts and their relationship to a larger form. The light but precise circular handwriting of the underdrawing establishes the relationship of spine to ribcage to pelvic girdle to limbs. Portions of the ribcage, the hind limb, and several spinal discs are brought sharply into focus with a heavier overdrawing. The still-evident under-drawing shows quite visibly through the more-detailed left hind limb, rendering the upper portion of that limb simultaneously solid and transparent. The hinging at the leg joint, the articulation at the pelvis, and the fusion of the ribs to the spinal col-umn are models of intense observation.

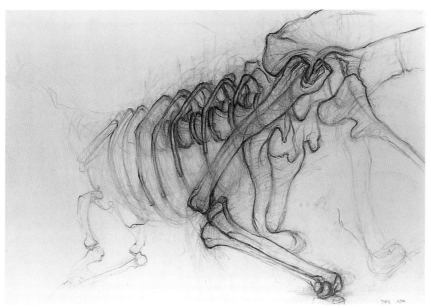

The two drawings focus on the dinosaur's pelvis and ribcage, describing each area's attachment to the spine, and also carefully consider the joints of the limbs. Figure 10 employs more decisive and singular lines to bring the pelvis into focus, while figure 11 uses the density of multiple lines and erasures (extracting the white of the ribs) to dramatize the view through the ribcage. The former incorporates the armature supporting the skeleton's structure as well as the hardware and wires that sustain the creature's posture, while the latter dismisses the hardware. This, together with the manner in which the darker lines graduate into the light underdrawing of the unfinished extremities, suspends the motion of the dinosaur in figure 11 in a cushion of space.

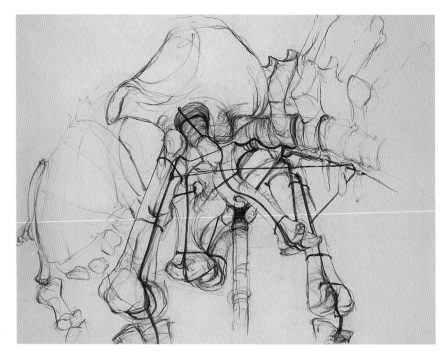

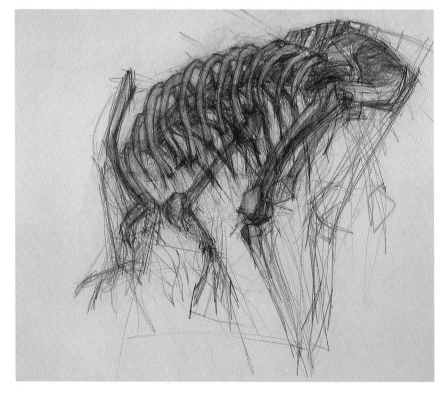

THE FIGURE AND
THE SKELETON

From the very first life-drawing session, there is a human skeleton in the studio as a visual reference so that the class is aware that the selfsame structure exists within the figure they are drawing. The 206—on average—bones that constitute the human skeleton are otherwise not paid much heed by students as they begin to draw from the live model. Indeed, if they were asked to give an accounting—disc by disc and rib for rib—the task would be daunting and discouraging. The actual act of drawing from the skeleton does not take place for several weeks. For the student of architecture, awareness of the skeleton is critical to the development of an analytic eye that sees past the curtain and mass of skin, sinew, and flesh to the bony framing—a structure that permits gesture and stance and provides the tools for locomotion and stability.

The skeleton in the studio hangs from the rotating arm of a wheeled stand so its position can be readily changed, albeit in its typical hanging posture. It can also be unhooked from the stand and placed and propped to correspond to the model's given posture during side-by-side, comparative poses. These exercises are interspersed with previously described studio exercises and continued over the course of the year.

EXERCISES

Quick Skeleton Studies. Turn the drawing pad horizontally, so that several skeleton studies may be drawn across the page. Draw the entire skeleton all at once, not bone by bone, moving the charcoal rapidly. Although the skeleton is linear in nature, think of the spatial volumes the bony structures encompass. Consider the oval volume described by the rib cage, the bowl-like space contained by the pelvis, the intersecting ovals of the front of the skull underlying the face, and the portion of the skull that is housing for the brain. Observe the serpentine twist of the spine. Change the skeleton's position every 5 minutes. (Later in the semester increase the time to between 10 and 15 minutes. At this point study portions of the skeleton more closely—skull to ribcage or pelvis to toe digits.) Vine charcoal. 24" x 36" newsprint (18" x 24" minimum).

Quick Side-by-side Figure and Skeleton Studies. Follow the same instructions as

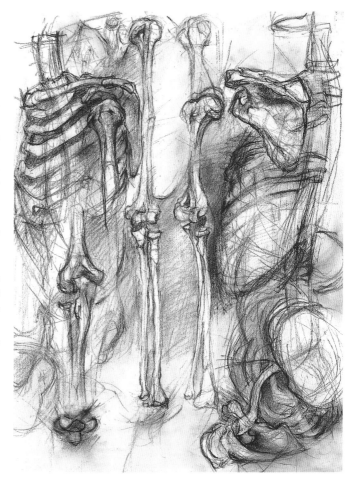

FIGURE 1

above. Begin by allotting 10 minutes per pose. In a week or two, abbreviate poses to 5 minutes. Draw the figure and skeleton together—again, in an all-but-simultaneous manner—in drawing them together the eye will become accustomed to darting from one form to the other and measuring their relative positions spatially. Avoid the tendency to complete first one figure and then add the other.

Longer Side-by-side Studies. After some weeks, depending on class progress, lengthen the duration of the exercise to between 20 and 30 minutes. Examine portions of the model's body and skeleton in greater detail, giving particular attention to articulation—knees, elbows, shoulder, etc. (Skeletal articulation is the configuration of two or more bones at a joint, which enable its motion.) It is good practice to draw such detailed areas within a larger context. Hence various studies might be made from skull through shoulder girdle and spine, from skull to ribcage, or from ribcage to pelvis, or from pelvis to toe digits, with the target area, such as the knee, being brought into sharper focus. Always keep the drawing hand moving from the live model to the skeleton and vice versa. Vine charcoal or charcoal pencil. 18" x 24" (or larger) newsprint.

Blind-contour Drawing. Follow the method for blind contour previously described in the bell-pepper assignments (see pp. 21–23). Begin at any point on the skeleton and let the pencil travel wherever the eye leads. Relatively hard sharpened pencil—H to 2B—on white paper. About 1 hour. (In the next week's exercise, start the blind-contour drawing at some other point on the skeleton.)

Blind-contour/Negative-space Drawing. Use the same drawing method and materials as above but with the following difference: examine the spaces between the bones rather that depicting the bones themselves. This is an especially useful tool in considering the interstitial spaces of the ribcage. These negative spaces between the ribs create a latticework in the drawing as ribs seen in the foreground visually cross over those that curve behind. Begin at any point and stop in an approximate hour. (Note that in blind-contour drawing proportion is *not* an issue. The result is frequently oddly disproportionate as the eye and hand slowly track one line at a time.)

The Skeleton Within the Figure. After two or three sessions of side-by-side drawings, view the live model's posture next to a similarly positioned skeleton and place

The skeleton was rotated and stopped in fixed positions. The overlapping study is of the upper portion of the skeleton—although a faintly drawn, suspended limb and the bones of an arm and hand to the right suggest axes around which the circulating skeletons turn. Several lightly sketched positions overlaid by darker studies add to the sense of rotation, depth, and transparency. In each of the overlaid studies, particular portions are brought into focus—in one the skull, in another the shoulder girdle, in yet another, the spine.

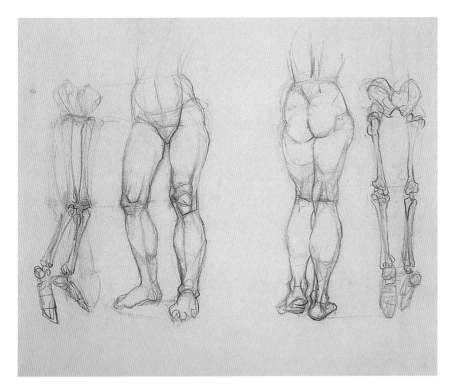

Figures 3 and 4 study the skeleton in relation to the fleshed out figure.

FIGURE 3

The drawing examines the lower portion of the skeleton and figure in like postures, noting the necessity and influence of the bony structure on the body's stance. Prominences of bone become evident at pelvis, knees, ankles, and feet.

the drawing of the skeleton within the volumes of the figure being studied. Begin the session with 40 to 50 minutes of the more rapid exercises described above. Next pose model and skeleton in proximate, similar postures—there might even be some overlap of bone and limb. Draw them as they are spatially related to one another. Now, on a new page, draw the figure and skeleton overlaid. Do not draw the figure first and then insert the skeleton. The process should be simultaneous. Vine charcoal on 18" x 24" (or larger) newsprint. 1½ to 2 hours.

Note: After the above exercises have been practiced for some weeks, the skeleton becomes a regular additional form in the longer two-model poses. It is an intriguing subject on its own and a constant reminder of the fundamental human structure.

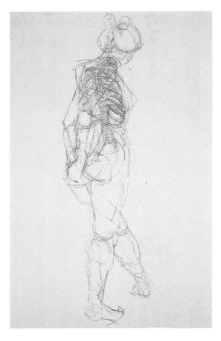

FIGURE 4

The drawing describes the ribcage within the contours of a fully fleshed-out figure. The light marking that sculpts the body aids the drawing's see-through illusion; solid and void are discussed in the area of the ribcage. The space that the curving ribs encircle is visible, yet the drawing presents a solid volumetric body.

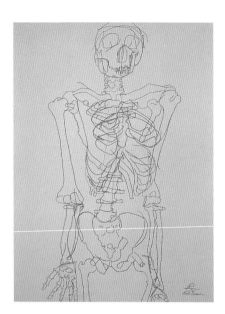

FIGURE 5

This classic blind-contour study displays the quirky distortions that result from maintaining the gaze chiefly on the object being drawn and only infrequently viewing the paper. Here the observant eye has tracked the stacking of spinal disc on disc, the variety of negative shapes created by the ribs' complex curves, the articulation of the elbow joints, even the jagged diagonal fissures that indicate the hollows of the eye sockets.

FIGURE 6

Model and skeleton share the model platform and seem to have traded roles. The model, doll-like, slumps forward; the skeleton sits pertly erect. These postural contrasts lend the drawing visual wit. Several layers of structural metaphor are represented: the platform supporting the two figures, the implicit skeleton supporting the model's body (notice the bony prominences in the face, knees, ankles), the clothing falling in planar folds from the support of shoulders and rib cages. Design is structured: the page is parsed into a series of supporting rectangles—platform, cube on platform, panel of wall—a motif that continues through the drawing of the skeleton and model.

LESSONS FROM THE MASTERS: HOMAGE AND REINVENTION

Art is built upon other art. For centuries, artists and architects have learned from and celebrated the work of their antecedents and their peers. Drawing is the very means of this research. Michelangelo, born some fifty years after Masaccio's death, made studies from his frescoes. Rubens drew from all the Renaissance masters, as his student van Dyke drew from him. The only record we have of Leonardo's destroyed *Battle of Anghiari* is Ruben's pen-and-chalk study of it. Rubens drew from Raphael, and earlier, Raphael, in his fresco depicting the School of Athens, paid tribute to his revered senior colleagues Michelangelo and Leonardo, dramatically portraying them in this composition.[1]

The list of architects who participated in the design of Saint Peter's in Rome (1506–1625) is a roll call from the high Renaissance. The visions of Bramante, Raphael, and Peruzzi, among others, were crowned by a dome Michelangelo had designed, which was inspired by Brunelleschi's dome in Florence.[2] Gaudí's consummate masterpiece, the Sagrada Família in Barcelona (begun in 1882 and still not complete), was a work already two years under construction when Gaudí was brought in to collaborate with Francisco de Paula del Villar. Villar resigned and Gaudí continued on for the rest of his life.[3]

Mary Cassatt was enraged by the rejection of her painting *Little Girl in a Blue Armchair* from the American section of the 1878 Paris Exposition Universelle. She was particularly piqued since her close friend and much-admired colleague Edgar Degas had "even worked on the background."[4] She perceived the rejection as an affront to the both of them. Picasso famously borrowed from everyone. His folio of lithographs drawn from

Velásquez's *Las Meninas* is but one instance of his appetite for the work of others.

The following exercises invite students to look back to the works of the past to inform their developing understanding of drawing. The master studies should not be considered attempts at forgery but a means of investigation. To a greater or lesser degree, the students reinvent the work and make it their own.

ASSIGNMENT

Select images from a master in which the work of the hand is clearly visible. Avoid reproductions with many blurred or indistinct passages. Repeatedly practice details of the drawing that exemplify the original artist's handwriting before attempting to reproduce the entire drawing. This "fool around" page made of bits and pieces of drawing should also be an investigation of

FIGURE 1

Study after Caravaggio.
Judith Beheading Holofernes,
c. 1598.

55

FIGURE 2

Study after Leonardo
da Vinci. Title unknown,
1510–13.

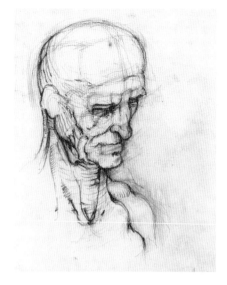

Make an underdrawing of the drawing in the spirit of the rapid figure sequences practiced previously. Allot no more than 2 to 5 minutes for this (see "Monkeys," pp. 43–50).

Make a separate rapid underdrawing, this time as the underpinning for a longer study of 20 to 30 minutes. Follow the master's hand respectfully but at the same time freely and with speed—not line for line.

Redraw the previous image at a larger scale, up to twice its original size. After this, make another enlargement, this time more interpretively. A change in drawing medium is usually helpful. Any medium on any paper. 30 to 45 minutes.

In an additional final drawing, "collaborate" with the chosen artist but reinvent the masterwork. In this drawing a further change in medium and scale is strongly recommended. Any medium on any paper. I hour or longer.

the design of the page with concern for negative space and passageway through the page. (As the fragments of drawing accumulate, arrange them in a way that gives the page a major gesture or spine.)

FIGURE 3

Derived from Albrecht Dürer's *Portrait of Dürer's Mother*, the study provides a classic example of a response to the first exercise in this series. The lines weave together the profiles, the jaw line, the carefully studied eyes, and an aging neck, combining these elements to create an intriguing ambiguity of positive and negative intervals and volumes.

Figure 4 *left*

The study of Rembrandt's *Elephant* gives the enlargement portion of the assignment an original twist. In the design of the page, the two larger elephants are superimposed in a transparent fashion, one above the other. The two larger studies seem to levitate above the firmly positioned smallest elephant, with its feet planted securely at the bottom edge of the paper.

Figure 5 *right*

The drawing presents a freely executed collaboration with Manet's *Mlle. V en costume d'Espada.* A number of spatial liberties have been taken. In a cunning reworking, the figures of the foreground toreador and the picador in the middle ground (in profile) are conflated. Their shared body conjoins opposing postures, achieving a balletic spin around a central axis. The arc described by the toreador's hands is greatly expanded, enhancing the balletic movement. A transparently rendered cape reveals the toreador's enlarged left hand and forearm, which press toward the viewer as if breaking through the picture plane. The swirl of the cape, with its incised and erased marks, elevates the drama of movement. The two dark hats meld with the rectangular shape of the stands to frame the two faces; the three-quarter face looks back at us with a confident gaze.

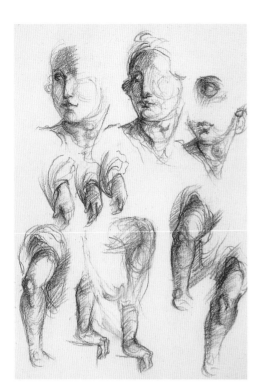

Figure 6 *left*

In examining Raphael's *Study for the Phrygian Sibyl*, the author makes multiple attempts to conquer aspects of the head and arms. Notice that in each of the series, no two attempts are identical—each is drawn freely to gain understanding of aspects such as the twist of the neck, the set of the eyeball in the depth of its socket, the complexity of the elbow's articulation, the pressure of the arm on the heel of the hand, the grasp of the fingers on the ledge.

Figure 7 *right*

The drawing presents several studies from Andrea del Sarto, creating from them a composite arc. This arc is enhanced by the layered dark tones employed to bring portions of each figure to a higher degree of finish. Of particular interest is the evolution from the transparent light marks of underdrawing to the build up of darker hatching, together with incised contour lines that more fully realize the body's volumes and features and explain the drapery of fabric.

THE DUMB OBJECT

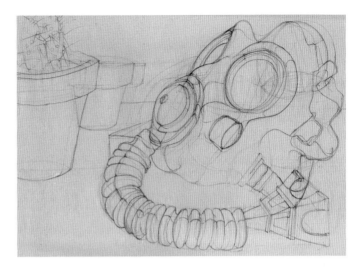

The dumb-object drawing exercise opened my eyes to simple observation, which has been helpful to me in my architectural work ever since. Careful examination of the forms and spaces, shaped by time, use, and natural forces often reveals something much richer than anything I could have constructed just by thinking.

On the street I picked up a rusty piece of metal that had long ago lost its utilitarian value and purpose. Drawing it at full scale or even larger forced me to observe every aspect of it and invent ways of drawing the intricate differences in materiality, structure, and shape. Having only this one little subject for constructing a large drawing made it impossible to avoid the relationship between the object and space, the portion of the paper left blank, and how light fell on it and made this seemingly flat and insignificant object into a rich, surprising form. — ANNE ROMME

The "dumb object" falls beneath conventional aesthetic radar. Often intimate to insignificant in scale, it is not valued as subject matter worth commemorating in drawing. In the 1960s and 1970s, artists Claes Oldenburg and Jim Dine brought the dumb object to prominence with their renditions of clothespins, lipsticks, screwdrivers, bathrobes, and other such objects. They were not the first to do this. John Peto and William Harnett, Pablo Picasso and Georges Braque all relished the ordinary and overlooked. In 1817 William Hazlitt wrote that Rembrandt "took any object, he cared not what, however mean soever [sic] in form, colour, and expression, and from the light and shade which he threw upon it, it came out gorgeous from his hands."[1]

Drawing from the dumb object is introduced at the same time as the handwriting and master-studies assignments (see pp. 40–42 and the preceding pages). It is an adjunct and not a separate assignment in itself. The dumb object is drawn intermittently through the balance of the program. Tracking the same, self-chosen item as the year unfolds aids the student in layering new concepts and skills. Its utility is in how it widens the eye, causing it to stare at the world and always to look for the visual surprise.

FIGURE 1

ASSIGNMENT

Choose as your object something you would previously never have thought of drawing. Let the drawing be influenced by the concepts that you are working with at the time. Draw this object with any medium at any size in any manner and scale and for any period of time.

FIGURE 2 *right*

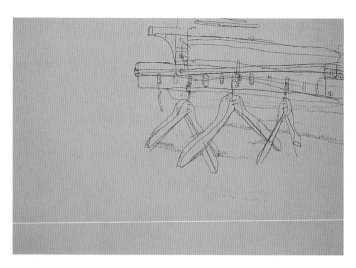

At first glance this blind-contour drawing seems to be a breezy offhand study of an ordinary circumstance: three hangers suspended from a utilitarian rack. However, the careful eye and hand of the artist has here commented on significant details and points of joining. The zigzag rivets that marry their two halves together show that the hangers are of wood. The rack appears to be metal because the slender depth of its members contrasts with the hangers' more substantially thick shoulders, and the bolts and joining details present further evidence. The sophisticated occupation of the upper right portion of the page suggests a likely corner location in a room or closet. Each hanger is suspended at a different angle, yet optically they cross each other in the drawing, sharing an animated gesture.

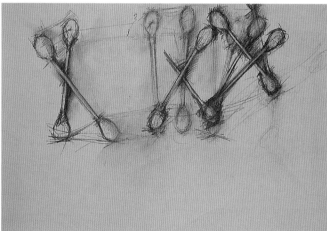

Figures 3 and 4 echo the Figure in Motion exercise (see pp. 30–34) in which each posture the model takes changes somewhat from the previous one.

FIGURE 3 *left*

Several Q-tips were placed and drawn, then one or two were repositioned and drawn again. Light markings that chart the negative space seem to measure and guide the tips' next positions and provide an underlying structure to the plot. The emphatic charcoal markings on some of the tips and sticks contrast with lighter, almost negligent markings on others, alluding to an object momentarily at rest and then in motion. The overhead—or plan—perspective creates the illusion that the Q-tips are laid on the very page the viewer is observing.

FIGURE 4 *right*

By contrast, the continuous hooked-curve, conga line-like placement and the incrementally changing scale of the pencil shavings create an illusion of depth. The detritus of charcoal bits and powder provides another level of visual wit. Tone, employed to indicate shadow on these tiny objects, connects the fragments, enhancing a curving spinelike gesture.

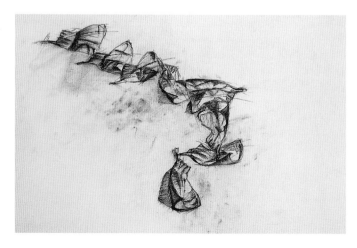

The drawings in figures 5 and 6 study ropes, each with a different strategy.

FIGURE 5 *right*

A centrally positioned coil with lines of rope escapes to the right, left, and bottom of the page. The coil was worked and reworked to a velvety darkness, with glints of light catching the twist in a whirling motion. The peripheral chords twirl away from this implicit spin.

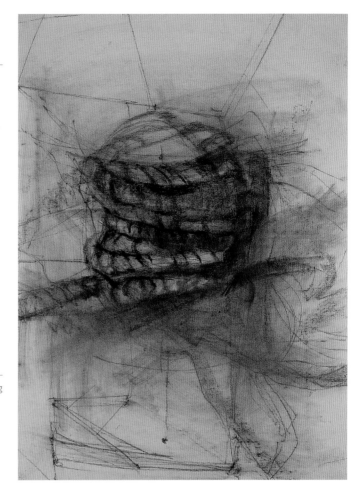

FIGURE 6 *below*

A length or two of rope is looped about as if being knotted or tangled. The employment of both hard and soft focus imparts a depth of field to the work: the darker, more-detailed areas come forward as the lighter, less-detailed areas recede. This lends an undulating motion to the ropes that a breeze might generate—rather than the sprung energy of a coil.

FIGURE I

PAPER BAGS

The paper bags assignment was the most difficult for me. I loved drawing the figure, but there was nothing immediately inspiring about paper bags. They were dull, ordinary things with no particular form. Later I figured out that one has to invent the figure in lifeless objects.

The first time we presented our paper bag drawings, most of us had basically made renderings of them. After drawing the bags for several weeks, those first, flat, graphic, illustrative drawings seemed

superficial. The later drawings were much more architectonic; this made them more compelling and alive. It is a very tricky thing to do. — DANIEL WEBRE

The paper bag is a singularly felicitous object to present to architecture students. Through a sequence of assignments its subtle virtues become increasingly obvious. Paper bags are readily available and come in an endless variety: serviceable brown kraft paper or plain white or colored; saw-tooth edged or straight-cropped at the top; crisp brand new or used and abused, with multiple wrinkles, creases, and twists. Printed on or plain, they range from upscale shopping bags to the standard-issue tan ones. They run the gamut of rectilinear ratios and can stand, stack, recline, or be made to lean rakishly at an angle. They are containers that, at once, define volume and void, dumb objects that usually fall beneath aesthetic consideration.

The paper-bag sequence is introduced at the end of a series of exercises concerned with developing a tonal handwriting; the students have been drawing upon master works in the previous weeks. Such "handwriting" should, by now, be attempted freely. Initially, ask the class to draw the paper bag as if in the hand of a Renaissance or Baroque master (pp. 55–58).

ASSIGNMENT
WEEK I
Select a minimum of five paper bags and arrange them, perhaps by a random toss. Consider what the page frames and rearrange certain bags, if necessary. Draw five relatively quick studies. Include all five bags within the confines of the page, though one or two might be cropped by the limitations of the paper's dimensions. Proceed with the eye and hand moving rapidly from one bag to another, considering negative space and

major planes on the bags' facades. Block in two or three major shapes of tone early on, considering the shape of shadow and cast shadow and the graphic pattern such shapes create. Compose each drawing differently, either by rearranging bags or by changing the point of view. Charcoal. 18" x 24" (or larger) newsprint. 10 to 15 minute duration per drawing.

Blind-contour Drawing. Include at least two bags, one in its entirety. Move the line from exterior to interior contour throughout the drawing process. Be alert to the concept of editing, such as which lines define the major planes, which lines provide coherent pathways through the drawing. With keen observation the "papery" quality of the bag and its materiality will emerge in this exercise. 1 hour duration.

Freestyle Drawing. Consider one of the first five rapid studies a sketch for the composition of this drawing. Any medium on any size or tone of paper. 1 hour minimum.

WEEK II

Repeat the drill described above with the following changes:

Arrange the bags so that the top or bottom of two or more is at eye level, with the remaining bags below eye level. As an alternative, position all bags at eye level.

Blind-contour Drawing. Focus on the negative space between the bags. Draw the shapes of all five (or more) bags, at least in part. Explore some minor aspect of the bags' interior creases. 1 hour.

Freestyle Drawing. Consider negative space and the abstract pathway that the shape of tone creates on the surface of the page. 1 hour.

Note: At the critique of these drawings, slides are shown of Raphael's tonal studies for his Vatican Stanza fresco, The School of Athens, in the Stanza della Segnatura, Rome, Italy (1510–11). The entire composition is presented as well as details of the various figure groupings in their hierarchical positions on the broad expanse of stairs.

WEEK III

The exercises assigned for this week follow the format of the two previous weeks, but now position the bags at eye level and above, or entirely above. This phase engenders great ingenuity in staging the location of the bags: they may be taped to the ceiling, suspended from strings, or simply placed on high shelves or stacked boxes.

FIGURE 2

Although based on the blind-contour method, the drawing does not strictly adhere to it. (For a classic rendition, see "Bell Peppers," p. 22.) In this drawing, the twists and shifts in the postures of each bag are cunningly revealed. The horizontal bag at bottom right assumes an uncanny body-like gesture, inviting the viewer into the middle ground, where three upright bags are grouped together and one stands apart. Keen observation and range in line weight indicate major and minor folds and wrinkles. Editing comes into play as particular planes are left quite free of wrinkles, contrasting with more detailed areas. The bags are positioned below eye level.

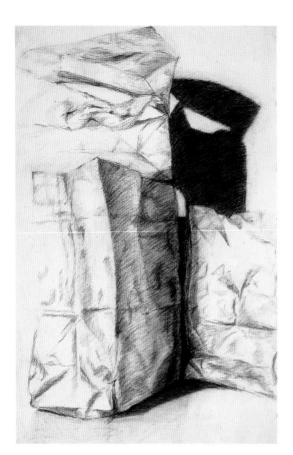

FIGURE 3 *left*

The crease line that designates the top quadrant of the bottom left bag hops to the top of the bag to its right and indicates eye level. The design strategy is noteworthy. The clever stacking of bags at top left and dramatic use of a dark shadow create the illusion of two closely positioned towers. The dark shape between the vertical bags emphasizes the sliver of negative space between, and the shadow on the wall reveals an eye-shaped cutout, paired with a similar eye shape to its left; the drawing peers back out.

FIGURE 4 *below*

The drawing takes a lively interest in the scale and fabric of a total environment. The top of the table marks a horizon, placing the bags themselves just above eye level. The curved line at the bottom foreground leads the viewer to the plane where the bags cavort, and the cursive handwriting dancing across the drawing further enhances their combined gesture. The dark tone on the two left windows is a backdrop for bags on the left and engages two bags at the right before continuing down the angled table supports. Here line and shape are deftly woven together.

FIGURE 5 *above*

An example of a quick study, the drawing presents five bags sharing one gesture. Moving from left to right, four of them tip rakishly against one another, pushing against the fifth horizontally collapsed bag. Bold handling of the charcoal invests the drawing with lively energy and reflects the loose handwriting developed in the rapid figure-drawing exercise. A bold massing of dark tone moves from planar shadows on the surface of the bags to the shape of their shared cast shadow, making the bags' rightward spill all the more emphatic.

FIGURE 6 *right*

Chalk-whitened planes are pulled out from the dark charcoal/pastel worked ground. The major event (bags stacked on a stool) takes place at the left of the page, giving the right "empty" portion of the page an independent weight. This empty, or negative, space is interrupted by a dark oblique triangle at the bottom right, indicating the perspective of the wall, tilted away from the picture plane. The angled wall, which at first seems frontal, works in accordance with the varied angled positions of the individual bags while the white lit planes on their surfaces weave the bags together into two major groupings. The cropping of the bags by the paper's edges provides further drama as the bags appear to press forward in front of the plane of the paper.

1927—make the clearest argument for analyzing organic form by slicing, planing, and cubing it. For the student of architecture this is of particular interest as a visual exercise in reconfiguring and reconstructing what meets the eye.

Giacometti—particularly in his drawings—stood at the crossroads between the great traditions of Western art and the new directions to which twentieth-century Modernism pointed. These drawings done in the early 1920s—his own years of study, formation, and early development—deserve the student's attention. During this period he made studies from the nude, portrait heads, and still lifes in which he employed a curiously speculative and yet precise manner of marking the shape of his subjects into a series of planed slices to investigate the turns and shifts of their subtly complex forms. Although not a new artistic device, Giacometti's use of the plane made transparent the dialogue between the mind and eye. He brought to the method a unique aesthetic force; he brought to the human form a geometric and architectonic translation.

ASSIGNMENTS

There is compelling logic in placing Giacometti and planar drawing after the paper bag assignments. The paper bag is an object composed essentially of imagined planes, which is useful to highlight the issue of editing—of choosing the most essential planes—rather than sculpting form from planes. It is in decoding the planar possibilities of rounded forms that reference to Giacometti is most relevant. The following exercises are often presented conjointly with flower and shoescape assignments (pp. 70–80) and the weekly studio sessions of drawing from the model. Slides and reproductions of this phase of Giacometti's drawing oeuvre are shown in

FIGURE 1

A studio drawing from the live model clearly reveals the collaboration with the master. While there is evidence of planar exploration on the figure itself, the chief focus here is the garment that wraps and defines certain volumes of the body. The transparency of the fabric serves to explain, rather than to conceal, the figure beneath its folds.

GIACOMETTI AND PLANAR DRAWING

From Luca Cambiaso to Pablo Picasso, from Paul Cézanne to Francis Bacon, the concept of the plane has been an invaluable tool in comprehending and decoding curved and complex volume. While the works of these and numerous artists provide excellent examples for students of drawing, the early drawings of Alberto Giacometti (1901–1966)—those completed between 1919 and the first week—together with an overview of his career—to emphasize his early planar approach.

WEEK I

Obtain an apple or a pear, or both. Cut the skin away in flat distinct slices, not in a long continuous peel that mimics the fruit's round contours. When this is complete, the fruit is no longer a round object; now its surface is covered with planes. Place the fruit in a situation with strong light from one direction—this will aid in differentiating the planar slices. Do not "tile" the fruit by marking in each individual plane one at a time. Draw the fruit rapidly—10 minutes per study. Change the position of the fruit. Draw again. Charcoal, charcoal pencil, carbon pencil. Any paper.

Browse through several reproductions of Giacometti's early figure drawings. Do a Fool Around page (see "Master Studies," pp. 55–58) in which you draw portions from one or several drawings. As you freely practice patches of Giacometti handwriting or small portions from his drawing, consider how these will link up with other portions and how areas of negative space might begin to emerge. Same pencils as above but no vine charcoal. Keep pencils sharp so that line quality will remain distinct. White or hard surfaced paper. 20 to 30 minutes.

WEEK II

Drawing 1. Repeat the Fool Around study this time using only one specific Giacometti drawing. **Drawing 2.** Using the same reproduction, do not attempt a copy of it, but draw your own drawing as though working from the live model. Do not draw part by part. Draw freely but respectfully for 5 to 10 minutes. **Drawing 3.** Draw your own version once again, keeping your handwriting light; this is an underdrawing. Upon this same drawing, continue to layer and build a more careful study of Giacometti's drawing, marking in tonal hatching. Differentiate between light lines and those that are more emphatically marked. The scale of the drawing should not be remarkably larger than the reproduction from which you are working. Same media as Week I. 30 to 45 minutes.

WEEK III

Choose another of Giacometti's geometrically planed figures. Repeat the methods of Drawing 3 of the previous week's exercise. Do another drawing at least twice as large—or even much larger. Use a different and bolder medium—soft or compressed charcoal, pastel, oil bar—on a rougher-surfaced paper. Do not draw from the reproduction. Draw from your own previous study. Keep Giacometti in mind but draw quite freely, as though you are collaborating with him.

Note: During these same weeks, students are encouraged to draw from the model in studio sessions as though in collaboration with Giacometti. Later in the first semester and again and the end of the academic year, when portraits are assigned, Giacometti becomes a resource in planing the landscape of the face and head.

FIGURE 2

A trio of studies considers pairs of pears, discovering with a delicate hand how the surface cuts assist in analyzing roundness. Progressing from left to right, the studies become increasingly sensitive to the interdependence of the two forms. A darker line links the pears in the middle study. While some aspect of transparency is suggested in this study, it becomes most evident in the right-hand coupling. Similarly, variations in the lightness or darkness of lines that define the fruits' outer contours close or open each fruit's boundaries, allowing the space of the page to enter the density of the flesh of the fruit.

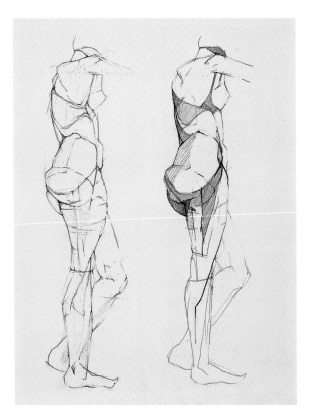

Reproductions of Giacometti drawings inspired
these studies. Figure 3 (left) is a faithful two-part
study, while figure 4 (below) is freely drawn,
departing from the actual text. While the first
is not a slavish reproduction, it is a thoroughly
respectful study, immediately calling to mind the
original drawing. The drawing below, however,
pushes past the master to present the student's
own internal predilections. The body forms are
softened and more voluptuous and erasure has
been applied more loosely, referring to the quality
of light as much as to plane. Neither rendition
forgets its debt to Giacometti.

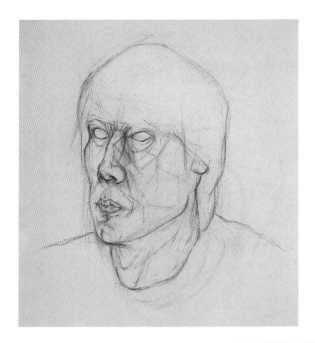

FIGURES 5 AND 6

These drawings are done after studying Giacometti's geometric portraits and heads from between 1920 and 1937. Neither drawing addresses the iris of the eye, lending them the same curiously blind gaze one finds in archaic Greek sculpture. Notice in both the darker line weight, which in figure 5 (above) begins to define a center axis (often present in Giacometti), while in figure 6 (right) it makes the eyeless gaze emphatic. Each drawing treats the mass of hair as flat negative space, but a light line discovers the contour of the skull beneath the mop of hair in figure 6. Although accounting only for the head and neck, each drawing achieves a gestural quality by careful observation of the poise of the head on the column of the neck. In figure 5, there is a slight tilt of the chin upward, the gaze blankly peering up rather than out; the neck in figure 6 twists as the head turns to gaze blindly at the viewer.

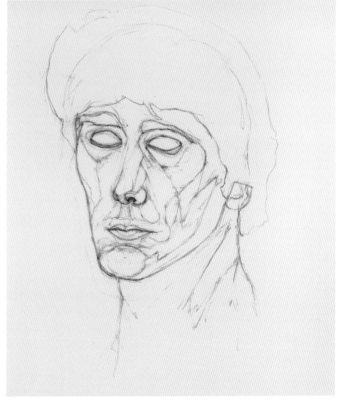

69

Figure 1

FLOWERS, PLANTS, AND MONDRIAN

If a single artist's work and philosophy could be cited as essential to the geometric aesthetic of twentieth-century Modernism, that artist would surely be Piet Mondrian (1872–1944), best known for his spare rectilinear compositions. Less known is that during the same period Alberto Giacometti employed the plane to reinvent the human form, Mondrian drew and painted—usually a blossom at a time—a folio of flowers that were a bouquet to observation. "I never painted… romantically, but from the very beginning I was always a realist," he wrote.[1]

A significant influence in Mondrian's early work was his Dutch countryman Vincent van Gogh (1853–1890). In van Gogh's flowers there is a fevered—yet structured—exuberance. Mondrian's flowers become increasingly ephemeral, yet structure persists. In the flowers of each of these artists a curved line is rarely encountered: sunflowers, irises, curly-headed dahlias, all are treated with the planed geometric slice. It is in Mondrian's fascination with dying flowers—his drawings of the angularity of their shriveling petals—that his use of the plane is most evident. For the student beginning to project structural language onto the delicacy of flowers, the preceding weeks' studies from Giacometti's cubed forms provide an invaluable guide to the parallel geometric inclinations in the flowers of Mondrian and his antecedent, van Gogh.

Note: In introducing the flower sequence, slides and reproductions of these three artists are shown.

ASSIGNMENTS

WEEK I (HOMAGE TO GIACOMETTI)
Obtain three stems of flowers with blossoms whose structural reading is evident—lilies, gladioli, tulips, daisies, dahlias are all good for this purpose. Consider the gesture of each stem and the gesture the stems make as a group. Draw the gestalt of stems and blossoms rapidly, not focusing on any single flower. Consider placement on the page so that the entire page is activated—though it need not be filled. Keep in mind that dead center is a conventional, although not necessarily the most compelling, choice. Vine charcoal or any easy-to-erase medium. 24" x 36" newsprint. Four drawings, each 15 minutes.

Giacometti Collaboration and Negative-space Study. Select the most compelling design from the initial exercise. In placing the underlying web of light marks that begins the page, give negative spaces the same attention you employ to draw the stems and blossoms. These negative shapes will lend variety and rhythm to the two-dimensional pattern created on the paper and will significantly aid in the measurement of each flower's spatial relation to the others. In analyzing the bends and turns of petals, leaves, and stems, employ planar slices. Charcoal pencil, carbon pencil, or HB-4B pencil. 24" x 36" white paper. 1 hour.

Freestyle drawing. Synthesize the drawing issues stated in the two problems given above. Also address the issue of focus by selecting an individual blossom area or passageway to elaborate with greater detail. Any medium. Any paper. 1 hour.

WEEK II (THE DYING BLOSSOM:
HOMAGE TO MONDRIAN)

Begin as above with fresh flowers. Then record how the flowers wither over the span of a week. Draw every two days: notice the change in the stem and its posture as well as the decay of the blossoms. Pay attention to the manner in which negative space varies—between petals, between leaves. To promote drying remove water from the container or remove the flowers from the water. A minimum of three drawings. Any medium on any paper. 45 minutes to 1 hour (or longer).

Note: At times potted plants may also serve as subject matter for these assignments.

FIGURE 2

FIGURE 3

A fluid rapid study of the shared gesture of three gladioli stems is set in the foreground. Their gesture is echoed and answered by the lightly sketched figure in the background. The water jar's left edge creates a central seam, picked up again above by the right stem's top line. The gladioli's shared leftward inclination is anchored back onto the page by the figure at the right.

Figures 4 and 5 each employ planar analyses in individual fashion.

FIGURE 4

The negative space is emphasized by tonal hatching, which occasionally enters the space of the petals and thereby attaches the petals to the ground of the paper plane. This tonal area is fairly rectilinear in shape and serves to halt the strong diagonal thrust that the lilies make toward the right upper corner.

FIGURE 5

Gridlike lines mark the spatial twists and turns of the plant's sturdy leaves, revealing an unexpected angularity at their points of bending. White chalk hatching at the left of the plant heightens the negative space. The same white highlights planes on the leaves to the right, linking the three-dimensional volume of the plant to the background flatness of the page. The shape of the white background enforces the suggestion of a rectilinear block defined by the plant's leaf ends and edges.

FIGURE 6 *right*

This is a quiet, elegant example of a negative-space/blind-contour drawing. Outer contours are more firmly defined while sparely used lighter lines trace the veining and bending of the leaves' surfaces, lending them a convincing dimensionality. Small interstices between stems and leaves are carefully examined.

FIGURE 7 *below*

A drooping gladiolus stem bends leftward from its water container. The paper frames its long-necked arc, while the container is somewhere offstage to the right. The bend of the stem's arc, articulated by dependent leaf spears, buds, and a wilting blossom, suggest a spine and ribcagelike grasp of the space at the bottom region of the page. Moving from the left tip of the stalk, tightly closed buds appear, then buds about to open, followed by the blossom to the right. The stalk's downward droop, the page's chief topic, speaks of decline. The drawing reads as a metaphor of the span from life to death.

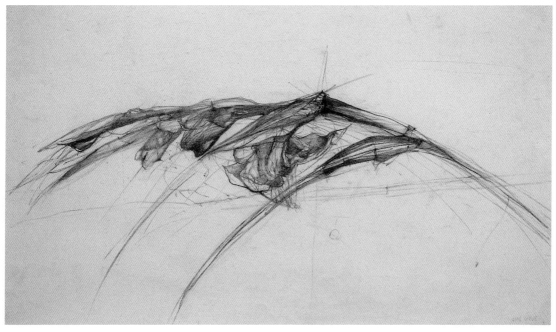

FIGURES 8 AND 9

The drawings attentively record the shriveling and dying of a lone daisy (or two) with a subtly nuanced line. The student draws with an empathetic response to the bent, twisted, and arched gestures of the fragile stems and sere petals. The analytic use of planes and space is entirely in the service of the drawings' whispered poetry.

Figure I

SHOESCAPES

*Having drawn since I was a child, I thought
I was pretty good until I took Sue Gussow's
drawing class during my first year. In one
of her exercises—drawing shoes piled up
on top of each other—I learned how to
observe. The nature of the object made you
look at both the interior and the exterior of
the shoe. The complexity of the total shape
forced you to look at the negative space
in and around the assembly. There were
folds in the leather to consider, how the foot
shaped the shoe by walking in it. This was a
very elegant problem that made you really
look. Drawing this everyday object gave me
the ability to draw complex assemblages of
objects, to consider space inside and out.
My mother, who is a painter and teacher,
loved this exercise and some others taught
in Sue Gussow's class so much she taught
them in her own drawing course.*

— JEE WON KIM

Akin to architecture, clothing provides shelter and enhances or announces culture, function, taste, and class. It could be argued that the shoe, beyond all other clothing, is the most architectonic in its structure and function. Standing atop a footing—the sole—built in adherence to a volumetric model—called the "last"—the shoe provides the foot, its occupant, with protection from climate and injury. An architect might well be intrigued by the construction—the anatomy—of the modern shoe. The shoe as we know it is a complex structure, and like the house it has acquired a special vocabulary to identify its structural members. Some of its elements are generally familiar: sole and heel, tongue and lacing. But most terms are not common to their wearers: the outer, the puff, the shank, the toe cap, the quarter, the vamp. It is, however, mainly the shape of the shoe, the void it encloses and the plane it stands on, that is the principal preoccupation of the Shoescapes assignments. Shoes present an excellent adjunct assignment to drawing from the human form; their convexities and concavities are modeled upon the foot itself.

In order to avoid a preoccupation with the shoe's surface attributes—the stitching, the lacing, the grommets—and to focus on the shoe's occupation of space, shoes will be examined not singly nor in pairs but in multiples—five or six shoes. In studying the group simultaneously, the primary concern will be devoted to the manner in which the shoes are placed to choreograph a space.

In addition to their allusion to function and fashion, male, female, or unisex, shoes come with yet another narrative attribute: they indicate direction. Even when independent of the foot and placed immobile on the floor, the shoe is a visual vector in the space: each toecap points to a specific direction. This guides the observer's eye across the field of paper on which the shoes are drawn.

ASSIGNMENT

Choose five or six shoes. Do not select brand-new ones; find shoes that show the imprint of a foot, the embossment of toes, wrinkles from wear. The foot's impression indicates dimensions of time and memory. The number of shoes in the assignment requires that you deal with a complex arrangement of several objects assembled in one space: consider movement and passageway across the field of the paper.

Toss several shoes randomly or manipulate them to form an interesting arrangement. Remember that it is one thing to create an exciting arrangement of actual shoes and quite another for this arrangement to become a good design on paper. Consider how the entire group will fit on the page. Read the group of several shoes as one creature with an implicit (invisible) connecting spine.

Draw four quick studies of all the shoes, drawing them together at once. Remember the implicit spine. Consider how the total configuration of shoes might best be placed on the paper—high, low, center. Hold back from focusing on details. Use the lines that best describe volume and plane. In each of the four drawings change either the shoes' arrangement or your own vantage point. Vine charcoal. 18" x 24" (or larger) newsprint. 15 minutes each, no longer.

Negative Space/Blind Contour. From the four studies choose the best composition. Draw the negative space surrounding the entire group of shoes. Look for narrow shapes of negative space that intervene between shoes placed at a small distance from one another. Think from the contour edge outward rather than focusing on the form of the shoe contained within the contour outline. Some light marks can be made, minimally indicating interior shapes, to test out the accuracy of the external contour, but keep the focus of the drawing on the exterior negative space. Use any drawing medium. 18" x 24" (or larger) white paper. 1 hour.

Freestyle Drawing. From the same composition chosen for the negative-space drawing, do a freestyle drawing but incorporate the following suggestions: employ areas of tone to address the issue of passageway, hatching in connecting shapes of tone to carry the eye from shoe to shadow to shoe. Shapes of tone may be employed to allude to the local color of a shoe—the level of gray that shoe might appear to be in a black-and-white photo. Local color can always be altered—or ignored—if that enhances the design of the drawing. Keep away from explicit detail until the later stages of the drawing. Detail is almost always the last strategy. Any drawing medium on any paper 18" x 24" (or larger). 1 hour.

The drawings in figures 2 and 3, both by the same hand, are clear examples of progress from a rapid study to a more fully realized drawing with a consciously chosen design strategy.

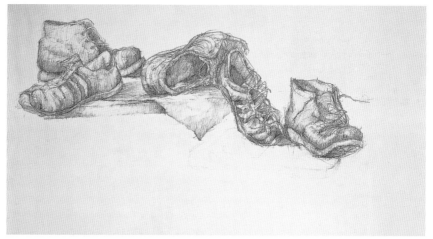

FIGURE 2 *top*

Thought is given to the gestalt and the placement on the page of the six randomly tossed shoes. They occupy only the top portion of the paper and march from top left downward to the white ground below. (Consider the paper with the bottom horizontal portion eliminated. The descending movement would be considerably diminished.) The two shoes with toe caps facing left counter and secure the compositional descent of the group of shoes to the paper. Planar slicing was employed to analyze the three-dimensional carving of the shoes; even their laces were drawn in planar fashion.

FIGURE 3 *bottom*

The drawing employs tone to indicate local color (the stripes on the running shoes), to model the form of the shoes, and to allude to cast shadows. Here the shoes are placed more consciously. Only one leftward-pointing shoe opposes the downward motion. (Notice one shoe from the previous study has been removed.) The increased buffer of white paper space enhances the drama of the group's movement. Apparent heel-to-toe connections create a "spine" that further enhances the shoes' shared thrust. The interior and exterior of the shoes are more fully explored here, as is the clear delineation of the top ledge of the wall of leather making up the shoes' openings— the housing of the foot.

FIGURE 4

The concept of this drawing is especially architectonic. The top of a centrally placed boot rises like
a tower in the center of several low-heeled
pumps, echoed by an auxiliary structure—a lower
black boot at its rear. All are lined up in parallel
profile with tension created by the backward-
facing white pump. The fairly abrupt cessation of
modeling in the white pump and in the tower of
the tall central boot links them to the flatness of
the white paper. This creates a spatial ambiguity
between the drawing's illusion of volume and the
flatness of the picture plane.

Figures 5 and 6 play with shoelaces as lines that extend the action of the shoes. In figure 5 the laces of two shoes tie the composition together in a tug-of-war. The laces in figure 6 lay casually away from the left-hand block the three pairs of shoes occupy. In the context of their design each drawing employs the shoelace to enhance a psychological statement. In drawing and design there is often the epiphany of unexpected meaning. This is another aspect of visual surprise.

FIGURE 5 *top*

It is the shoes themselves that march forward in lockstep, their up-turned toes adding animation to contradict the more static appearance of their profile "elevation." The tug from the left-facing shoe creates the warring tension, keeping the black boot's forward march anchored on the page. A playful tension between the paper's two-dimensionality and the drawing's three-dimensional illusion is created as the top edge of the page and eye level share the same line.

FIGURE 6 *bottom*

The placement of the shoes and the rendering of their wrinkles makes the viewer aware of their missing occupants held together in a close conversational square. The flowing laces echo what might be an unseen gesture of arms. The grouping at the page's upper left emphasizes the close proximity of the "occupants."

FEET AND LEGS

The challenge of drawing my feet became evident the third week of the assignment. How does one draw one's own feet week after week, I wondered. I learned to carefully look and to accurately see what was before me. I found that gravity plays an important role in how the masses of the feet relate to their context. I realized that the tendons, ligaments, connective tissues, digits of varying sizes, and bones all reveal themselves differently through the skin when oriented in different positions. Certain parts of the feet, ankles, and lower legs appear soft and rounded when restfully reclining on an ottoman, while the same anatomical elements are quite angular and planar when standing firmly in front of a mirror.

— CHARLES KREKELBERG

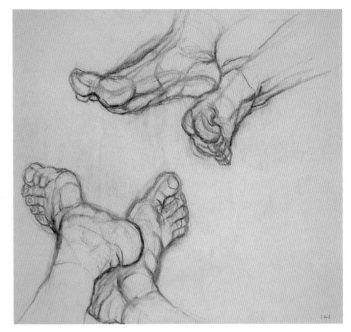

FIGURE 1

Feet are that portion of our extremities most distant from the eyes. Feet most often fall beneath our gaze. Save for the daily ritual of housing them in shoes (further obscuring them from view), we seldom take a serious look at them. Unlike our hands, with which our eyes are in constant collaboration, our humble feet are more typically called to visual attention when they cause us pain (fashion slaves excepted). When, for instance, was the last time you carefully examined the sole of your foot? Yet there they are—those feet—our base, our daily contact with the ground plane, with the earth.

When we speak of a firm footing, we refer to a stability of posture or a secure basis. In architecture the form called "footing" mitigates between foundation walls, interior columns (in larger structures), and the earth. Usually rectangular in form, typically composed of concrete, and larger than load-bearing columns, footings are thrust deep into the earth to establish a building's stance and stability.

The Feet and Legs drawing project evolved from the Shoescapes assignment. Although shoes had been discussed as structural housing for feet, many of the drawings pinned up for critique appeared to be studies done from new shoes. Their more prominent attributes were stitching, laces, grommets, straps; no foot seemed ever to have occupied them.

The in-class exercise required students to remove their shoes and take a good look (while drawing) at their feet—their feet undressed, their feet in socks, and finally their feet back in shoes. The resulting drawings, however well drawn, resembled amputations. Feet were abruptly terminated at the ankles or legs were severed arbitrarily at the calf or somewhere below the knees—inventory from a body-parts shop floating about on a field of white paper.

The project evolved further. Drawing longer portions of the leg entering the page from the top, side, or bottom of the paper's edge immediately interrupts and divides the field of the page, creating that intriguing dialogue between negative cutouts and positive rendered volumes. Studies of feet and legs taken from their mirror image did not present as challenging a perspective as actual feet and legs drawn by gazing downward or outward, where the unexpected shapes created by foreshortening come into play. One student presented drawings depicting her actual legs extended to a mirror so that one foot toed its reflection, creating a four-legged image and opening a virtual window to the space beyond the picture plane. The scheme was incorporated into further assignments.

ASSIGNMENTS

WEEK I

Draw three drawings of your own feet and legs, either mirror image or viewing actual limbs, each in a different posture: first posture, legs and feet unclothed and unshod; second, legs with feet in socks; third, legs with feet in shoes (and socks—or not). Legs should be drawn from somewhere above the knee and should enter the drawing from the edge of the paper. Use vine charcoal. 18" x 24" (or larger) newsprint. 20 to 30 minutes for each posture.

Consider the three previous drawings and choose the most interesting posture as a scheme for the final drawing. It will be useful to make marks on the floor (or chair, etc.) to indicate the position of your feet and legs. Bits of masking tape are good for this purpose. Begin the drawing with feet and legs naked. Use any easy-to-erase medium on a sturdy 18" x 24" (or larger) sheet of paper. About 30 minutes.

Put socks on your feet and then continue to work on the same drawing, resuming the same posture. (This is the reason that marking the placement of feet is necessary). After another 20 to 30 minutes, put on shoes and continue on the same page.

At each stage, erase only when the drawing becomes confusing. With each new layer, erasure may be necessary to clarify the drawing, but keep erasure to a minimum so that the transparency of the drawn shoes and the presence of feet are in evidence.

WEEK II

Draw from your actual feet and legs, not from a mirror image. This vantage point introduces the challenge of *foreshortening* (looking either downward or outward) in the various postures drawn. The goal of foreshortening is to create the illusion of projection forward. It is complex to carry out given the endless variations of posture the body might assume. It is achieved by an apparent compression of those volumes that recede from the observer's eye. Key to the process is the keen observation of unexpected shapes—both positive and negative—that the eye will encounter. Charcoal or other mutable medium. 18" x 24" (or larger, although larger is encouraged) newsprint. Three studies, 30 minutes each.

Select the best of these three pages as a starting point for a freestyle study. Any drawing medium on any paper 18" x 24" (or larger). 1 hour or longer.

WEEK III

Draw your actual limbs as you have done the previous week but also include their mirror image in the drawing. Be inventive with your three poses—i.e., one foot might engage the mirror image—and with how you position the mirror. Vine charcoal or any mutable medium on any paper 24" x 36" (or larger). Three drawings, 30 minutes each.

As during the second week, select the best of the three previous studies for a freestyle study. Any drawing medium. Sturdy paper, 24" x 36" (or larger). 1 hour (or longer).

The drawings in figures 2 and 3 respond to the first and last segments of the first week's Feet and Legs assignment. In a search for the complex shifts of form in the foot's shaping, the drawings present a loose-handed version of planar slices.

FIGURE 2

The drawing employs planes in carving the foot's reciprocal convexities and concavities.

FIGURE 3

The drawing reveals a layering, first of socks, then shoes. Through the layers of cloth and leather, transparency allows the viewer to glimpse the shoes' occupants. Both drawings describe the student's own legs and their reflected images. Note the contrast in the thickness of the limbs as the tilt of the mirror thins out the legs' dimensions. Notice as well the radial position of the feet as they fan out from the student's perspective—her line of vision penetrating the almost-touching pair of heels at the left.

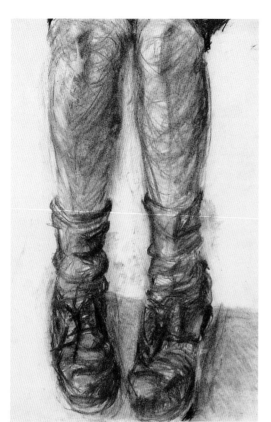

Figure 4 *left*

The drawing shows a straightforward mirror image of the student's fully dressed feet. Socks, wrapped about the ankles, echo the curved handwriting that describes the volumes of calves and knees. The assured rough charcoal marking describing the laces, wrinkles, and shoes speaks boldly of the feet inside.

Figure 5 *right*

Downward perspective dominates as the legs enter the page from the upper right corner. The foreshortened lower limbs enhance the sharp downward view. This thrust is anchored by the angled-foot position, which proclaims the floor plane. Turn the drawing upside down (or rotate it sideways with legs at lower right), and the spatial orientation in which it was drawn is apparent. Viewing it as presented is a more powerful design statement. It is useful in design and critique to turn work upside down or sideways to view it anew. Many design epiphanies occur in this way.

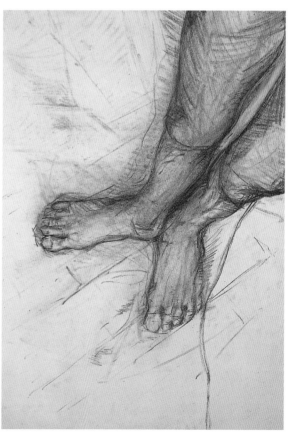

FIGURE 6 *left*

The mirror image expands the virtual space, opening it to the spatial realm beyond the picture plane. The actual legs, which enter the page from the bottom, come into the viewer's space in front of the picture plane. There are echoes of Giacometti and planar drawing in portions of the knees and feet—particularly useful in analyzing the underside of the reflected foot. The student wittily extends the toes of the reflected foot past the mirror's parameter to play with the toes of her actual foot.

FIGURE 7 *right*

The drawing weaves all aspects of the problems presented into a nude/sock/foot/shoe theme and variations, also adding issues of transparency and gesture. To the first underlying pose—one leg with a nude foot and the other encased in a knee sock—the student overlays a second shod posture. A light transparent handwriting in crossover places lends the legs a rhythmically kicking and rotating motion that rolls out and upward from the bottom left corner of the page.

CLUTTER

To draw clutter I explored domestic mess. Piles of clothes, compressed forms of materials and fabrics left in clumps after use—a dense amorphous mass amidst familiar, recognizable objects. Drawing would involve extracting visual connections from the crowded confusion of layered zones, to shape coherent figures from the sea of appearances that might merge and blend.

The recesses and nooks of clutter, its monads and folds, contain many shadows. Looking at the darkness, sorting through its quasi-invisible shapes, it is possible to uncover its order in degrees of black and ebony, dimness and shade. I drew spaces of unknown depth where the imagination roams. It is in the physical embodiment— with charcoal—of those dim zones that drawing takes place. The hand draws what the eye sees with no preconception of an a priori form, as if discovering, and in that act drawing approaches design.

As clutter embodies the opposite of empty space, it solidifies and makes tangible the invisible jumble of air, void, and pockets of air. The drawing of clutter starts as does the drawing of a still life yet transforms into a collection of noisy spaces and negative shadows. From the folds of a dress and the wrinkles of a shirt, trapped ghosts of space arise. In the drawing of clutter, the lurking appearances of darks, voids, and shades are tamed.

— TAMAR ZINGUER

It is from the humble particulars of our daily lives that larger abstractions may be formulated. In our observations we are confronted by a visual world of vast complexity and density. To reduce this agglomeration of color, texture, detail, and overlap to coherent imagery, we shape what we see. The clutter assignments grow out of a confrontation with visual density. How, in fact, do we shape what we see? How can we take this visual complexity and make it fit within a sheet of paper?

Quite the opposite of the traditional still-life problem in which ordinary objects are prearranged, the Clutter assignments confront the random haphazard pattern of things as they are found. The objective is to tease out a visual order or readability in an apparently disordered field. With the Dumb Object problem as its antecedent, the Clutter exercise trains the eye to search in unexpected corners for fresh imagery. It provides an antidote to dependence on received concepts of design and enhances visual inventiveness.

Clutter is not difficult to encounter. Some of its surefire locations are the tops of desks in a working studio, the bottoms of said desk drawers, the floors (and even the middle) of closets, the detritus on studio floors, corners in which odds and ends stack up and accumulate, and, of course, the kitchen sink. As the assignment extends over approximately three weeks, a number of sites may be visited.

ASSIGNMENT

Choose a cluttered or randomly placed condition. Do not improve upon it or move any object. You may, however, choose to move the frame or window through which this clutter—and occasional negative space—is viewed.

Cut two L shapes from a piece of cardboard and hold them together with paper clips to create the frame or viewfinder. The clips allow for a change in rectangular proportion ranging from square to golden mean to letterbox. Less precise, but always available, are the thumb and index fingers of your two hands. When held at right angles with one hand placed above the other, they create a box shape of rough determination

FIGURE 1

and indicate where on the page to locate critical shapes or patterns.

Draw a freehand rectangle on a sheet of paper. Inscribe it lightly so that it is subject to change. It may expand, close in, or change proportion as the drawing evolves. Leave sufficient margin around the drawn frame so that the design can expand in any direction. Inside the parameters of this frame, draw a geometric assessment of the shapes of the chosen view, aided by your frame. Initially draw the shapes primarily in line, perhaps adding one or two important shapes of tone.

Establish a focal area or two in the drawing—some detail or a place where lines that define objects and space converge. This may be something that caught your eye in the first instant, or the focus might emerge in the process of drawing. More sharply drawn lines or greater tonal contrast will point the viewer's attention at areas of focus.

Cluttered situations offer opportunity for invention in creating negative space. Opening the frame to include wall, table, or floor plane is one strategy. Another is the possibility of defining certain objects with only an external contour line and leaving them otherwise undescribed and blank.

Passageway is a crucial device in clutter drawings. Passageway can be achieved by emphasizing particular lines that travel from one object to another, moving from outline edge to interior delineation, in order to form intriguing visual routes. Allowing tonal areas to escape their inscribed boundaries and join one another in surprising ways can further create passageway—weaving the shadow on a object to its cast shadow or merging the tone of an object's local color to an adjoining shape of shadow.

WEEK I

Make four drawings of different clutterscapes, essentially linear. 20 to 30 minutes each. Make a fifth drawing introducing tone, taking more time. Allow the rhythm and texture of handwriting to stay vivid in the tonal areas. Pencil, charcoal pencil, carbon pencil on any paper. 45 minutes to 1 hour.

WEEK II

Make four drawings of different clutterscapes that introduce two or three major shapes of tone. 20 to 30 minutes each. Make a fifth larger drawing—possibly a blow-up of one of the previous studies—further developing tonal contrast, passageway, and focus. Same media as above on any paper. 1 hour.

WEEK III

Change the site to floorscapes and/or cornerscapes. Three 1-hour studies.

FIGURE 2

The frame encloses a distant view of the large studio in the School of Architecture. The visual jumble of receding table lamps, drafting boards, and casual mix of furnishing and personal paraphernalia is woven together by bold narrow areas of charcoal. These slender, dark rectangles link foreground and background in what seems one unifying gesture.

FIGURE 3

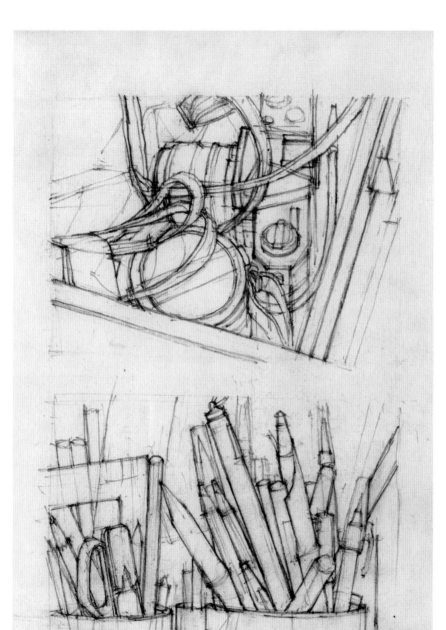

Two frames contain linear studies of clutter. The faint frames allow the edges of objects to become framing devices. At the top, two edges of the cluttered desk drawer form an angled parameter that points downward to the pen- and pencil-holders beneath. The reiteration of the drawer's corner by the angled staccato dance of the two overstuffed containers' occupants creates a dialogue between the two compositions. Light schematic measurement lines provide an underlay for darker contours. The varied line weights are more emphatic at points of meeting, creating a visual vibration. In these densely packed images, larger objects serve as negative space for the more tightly compacted smaller objects.

Figures 3 and 4 explore a closet's packed contents.

FIGURE 4

Areas of flat strong tonal contrast make a straight-forward case for creating positive and negative shape. Dark vertical areas move across the page in accordion folds and then descend at right to join an echoing horizontal path that stretches irregularly along the floor.

FIGURE 5

A second closet is viewed with more nuanced tonality. A dark pathway divides the drawing into three major areas. At lower left, this dark spine ascends diagonally to join a dark horizontal created by the garments' combined shadows at the center. The dark tone reaches up in a slim vertical stripe inside the closet, echoed by another slender dark rectangle at upper right. White shapes step diagonally from lower right to upper left and move through the lighter gray and white stripes of the suspended garments.

The line indicating eye level creates an organizing spine in figures 5 and 6.

FIGURE 6

A tipped pot and a spill of foreshortened flatware allude to a larger landscape. The outlined circumference of the pot suggests the sun or moon shedding light on the angled objects. Darkened punctures between the disordered flatware provide a spine along the horizon line.

FIGURE 7

Strongly contrasting areas define variously shaped containers placed tightly together. From a flat black cylinder at left, a dark tone joins a horizontal rectangle at the middle right. This conjoined dark shape reads as both background and foreground weaving through the drawing. Occasionally modified and modeled tone demonstrates volume while, frequently, the white, gray, or black areas are treated flatly. This creates an arresting *ambiguity* in which objects seem to be spaces and spaces assume volume.

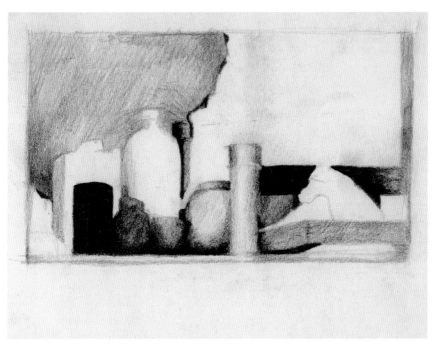

THE FIGURE
IN THE STUDIO

It is the function of architecture to design structures that define spaces to enclose, protect, and celebrate the gamut of human activity. Just as the seated figure and chair set up a relationship of measurement, the body—seated, standing, and supine—responds to and measures the space defined by the structures it occupies. The soaring immensity of a cathedral's inner space, the punitive narrow confines of a prison cell—these structures each consider the human body's scale, movement, and needs. The body is the architect's essential underlying module in conveying the implicit aesthetic and psychological intent of a structure. There is a reciprocity of measurement between body and building.

In weekly figure-drawing sessions, the models pose in a large studio cluttered with easels, stools, the odd chair, the detritus of other classes, and the scatter of clothing and supplies the students bring in with them. By the end of the first semester and certainly by the beginning of the second, the class has gained a measure of competence in drawing the human body, giving it gesture, volume, and stance and placing it on the page in a manner responsive to the shape made by the body's posture.

On a parallel track, at about the time when the class engages in the Clutter and Frame, Window, Room assignments (see preceding pages and pp. 100–11), they also explore the body in relation to the space it occupies—the walls, corners, furnishings, mirrors—the density and openness of daily life. From the beginning of the course two models are booked for each studio session so that no drawing momentum is lost when one of the models rests. In the longer poses, the models are frequently positioned together so that students develop the practice of drawing both bodies all-but-simultaneously and of understanding the negative space between them as vital to the design of the page.

Placing the models together with fabric, furniture, props, screens, and with mirrors that reflect and multiply the visual density creates a situation for the student to sort out and translate into a drawing that makes visual sense. Within this density, space must be created.

Note: The lone figure, centered or placed strategically on the page, is a compelling image. In order to place this figure in an architectonic context, notate—at minimum—a single other shape that locates the figure in the space of the room. Lone figure studies as well as the exercises described below will be practiced over the course of both semesters.

EXERCISES

Place the model(s) in a dense situation with randomly placed objects and furniture and carelessly tossed and draped fabric. Avoid a tasteful aesthetic arrangement.

A Scribble Study of the Entire Setting.
With vine charcoal draw a small rectangle on the page—approximately 9" x 12" or a little larger. Within this frame draw the entire situation rapidly, barely lifting the charcoal from the paper. Draw major shapes and pathways through the composition. Keep measurement in mind—not precise calibration but rapidly assessed and reassessed relationships. After the first 7 to 10 minutes, pause. Squint your eyes to see major shape configurations. Block in two to three major dark areas—no more. 3 to 5 minutes longer.

Framed Portions (Details) of the Entire Model/Prop Setting. Using two L-shaped cardboard pieces or the thumbs and index fingers of both hands, create a viewfinder. (See the Clutter assignments, pp. 86–91, for a detailed explanation.) Lightly mark a rectangle on the paper. This frame may be altered as the study progresses and as the composition demands more or less space. Do not merely frame head and shoulders as in a conventional portrait. Avoid placing one figure in the page's center, unless it is a compelling design strategy. Use broadly geometric shapes in plotting the composition (even for the shapes of the figures). Mark in major shapes of dark areas early on. Details—facial features, garment folds, hardware, etc.—may be added later as the drawing becomes more fully established. These framed studies may be on one large sheet of paper, provided the frames are a few inches apart. Charcoal or any easy-to-alter medium. 24" x 36" (or larger) newsprint, though single studies may be drawn on smaller sheets. Three or four studies, 15 to 20 minutes each.

A Long Framed Study. Choose the best of the above studies as the basis for a longer study. As you work, reevaluate the composition. Does it need more open white space? Might the frame be expanded to include more empty floor or wall? Consider which portion of the drawing might be pulled into sharper focus by means of cleaner edges, increased tonal contrast, greater detail. Establish a few major dark areas, then begin to consider the play of more subtle gray tones. Create passageway through the drawing by means of adjacent tones or lines that continue from one form to the next. Any easily altered medium on any paper 24" x 36" (or larger). 1 hour or longer.

Long Study of the Entire Model/Prop Situation. Begin with the small scribble study of the entire situation described above. Next, very lightly inscribe vertical and horizontal center lines, dividing the paper into quadrants. Begin lightly to mark in roughly geometric shapes that place figures and objects in their locations in the four quarters of the paper. Use tone to establish two or three significant dark shapes early in the drawing process. Always work back and forth, continuing to measure figures, objects, and spaces in relation to one another. Avoid embellishment and detail until late in the drawing process. Detail will occur organically as an adjunct of focus. Focus is best established after the underlying structure and design of the drawing are mapped out. Any medium on any paper 24" x 36" (or larger). 1½ to 2½ hours.

Multiple and Mirrored Figures. Placing mirrors in the models' setup not only expands the visual field, it also multiplies the number of figures. Reposition models from one place to another in 20- to 30-minute intervals to add to the dense configuration of the drawing. At the beginning of the time allotted for the drawing, pose the models in a setting together with two or more large (or varying sized) mirrors. As in the previous exercise, establish the entire composition on the page, avoiding the temptation to focus on one specific model.

A spatial arena must be established on the page for staging the several additional poses. After 30 minutes one model takes a break and assumes another posture. The other model continues in place for an additional 15 to 30 minutes, then breaks and moves to another position. The fixed model adds a consistent frame of reference for measurement and may establish a focal point for the drawing. Clothed students may enter the setting for 20-minute poses. Models might put on or shed articles of clothing as they change poses. Any medium on any paper 24" x 36" (or larger). 2½ hours.

FIGURE 2

A lone model stands solidly and monumentally high, her waist at about eye level, an arm akimbo, her feet planted firmly on the allotted cube. Her slightly counterpoised posture is heightened by the alternating distribution of the tonal shapes on her body from her head to her left arm (right on the drawing) to her right leg. While the drawing reveals a solidly sculpted body (the robe's fabric rendered transparent) the drawing also speaks boldly of location. At the bottom of the page the top plane of a cube enters the picture plane with an exaggerated tilt, creating a ramp upward to the centered cube supporting the model. Behind her, vertical panels enforce her classic stance and lightly but clearly locate her in a corner of the room, while the L shape of the baseboard at bottom echoes the ballet position of her feet.

FIGURE 3 *left*

The visible portion of two models' partly draped bodies and props employs two major shapes of dark local color that graphically punctuate the drawing. A series of echoing triangles create the drawing's underlying structure. Note the triangle created by the female model's right leg with the edge of falling fabric, a similar one above formed by the easel legs, and the sideways-turned triangle created by the male model's bent arm, repeated by his calf and the leg of a chair. As a result of the frame's cropping, a juxtaposition of triangles is pervasive in negative areas as well.

FIGURE 4 *right*

The model's back presents a baffle the viewer must look beyond to discover the legs and an arm of two other figures, fabric, and fragments of objects. Although her back is only slightly modeled (notice the shoulder blades and the drapery describing the volume of the hips), the light marking and erasure keep her shape essentially flat and transparent and visually on the same plane with the page's background flatness. She is defined and dismissed by the darkening of her contour edges and the prominence of the jagged fragment beyond her right edge. The shapes she partly obscures press forward toward the viewer's eye. Through these means the drawing achieves an intriguing spatial ambiguity.

Figures 5 and 6 reveal the model, skeleton, and an occasional student in multiple postures.

FIGURE 5 *above*

The drawing deals with the issues of spatial overlay and transparency. Some of the models' positions occur in the same location just occupied in a previous posture. A darker marking necessary to carve out secondary and even tertiary changes in both model and position appears over a light underlay describing the positions taken earlier in the span of drawing. This lightness and subsequent density of line work describing the overlap of poses suggests a time-lapse image, an illusion of continuous movement.

FIGURE 6 *right*

Lines that define the tall mirror's framing appear through the seeming transparency of the foreground model's body. Her crossed arms curiously disappear as the head of the male model seated behind her claims that space. The mirror frame's edge (in its earlier, lightly marked version) defines the vertical axis of the page. This line creates a sheer cut against which the background group of figures move forward while the central figure standing in the foreground presses back against that dividing line.

FIGURE 7

The model and the studio
are each given equal billing.
The angled skylight, its
framing, and the student's
upward perspective suggest
the studio as theater. The
diagonal lines describing the
skylight, lighting pole, and a
baffle activate a backdrop
that occupies more than
half the page. At the far
left is a fraction of the back
view of another model;
her head, shoulder, and the
chair back provide a three-
step scrim, beyond which
the male model sits. The
model directs his gaze both
out at the audience and left
toward the other model.
The student's upward
point of view—a theatrical
reference—is emphasized
by the upward curving lines
of the model's abdominal
wall.

THE STUDIO MOVES OUTDOORS

The spring semester begins in the dead of winter. As daylight lengthens and the caprices of early spring bring randomly splendid days, the class takes supplies and models and moves outdoors. This "open" studio presents a greatly expanded field of vision. It multiplies the visual density that must be framed and translated to the page.

For the student of architecture, it provides the challenge of scaling the figure to the urban setting. Two locations at The Cooper Union with immediate eye-grabbing appeal are the rooftop of the Foundation Building and a small Engineering Building patio that sports a couple of trees and is home to the sculpted granite eagle salvaged from the demise of the old Penn Station.

Figures 8, 9, and 10 weave into one tapestry the complexity of students engaged in drawing, a rooftop with its ductwork and housings, and more distant city view and sky.

FIGURE 8

The foreground and middle-ground figures hunched over their drawing boards echo the blunted cone shape of the ventilation cap. The truncated arch of the large duct at the page's center (mirrored by a second duct to the right) provides a dramatic foil for the group standing to its left. The pattern of strongly defined dark shadows created by the bright spring light ties the drawing together graphically. A distant building's windowed front facade, framed by the two ventilation ducts, is visually pulled into the middle ground as the shadowed side of the center duct joins the gray of the building's facade. The left edge of the same building's adjacent side and the left edge of the center duct are lightly defined, somewhat blending their shapes together and opening them to the drawing's background plane—the sky.

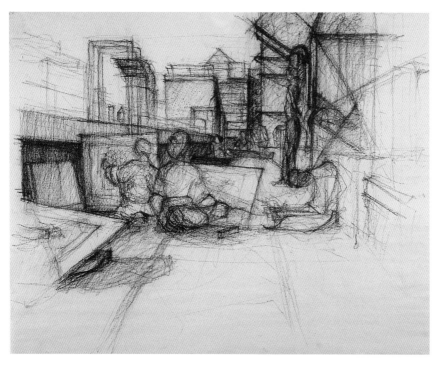

Figures 9 (top) and 10
(bottom) were drawn at
the same time from oppo-
site sides of the model,
presented as a minor
element in both of the two
works. The model can be
seen most clearly in figure
10, leaning, bare chested,
against a rail. The back- and
middle-grounds of figure
10 depict the propped-up
drawing boards placed in
the foreground in figure 9.
Similarly, the foreground
figure to the right in figure
10 appears small and lit
against the darkened
parapet in figure 9. Again,
piecing together the blend
of students, ducts, drawing
boards, and the geometry
of the roof's furnishings
provides the central impe-
tus of each work. In each
a compelling one-point
perspective carries the
viewer's eye to the middle
depth of the page, where
the juxtaposition of the
roof's housings and distant
buildings creates a visual
plane that parallels and
reasserts the flatness of the
picture plane.

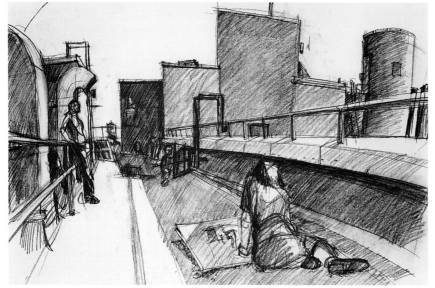

Figure 1

FRAME, WINDOW, ROOM

I. FRAME: LOOKING THROUGH A WINDOW

The concept of frame, first explored in the Clutter project (pp. 86–91), is expanded here. The window assignments advance the concepts of freehand (as differentiated from instrument-aided) perspective, consider problems of measurement and scale, and elucidate the abstract design possibilities inherent in the use of *tonal shapes*. The initial application of the window assignment—the framing of a view—brought many related drawing issues into focus and spawned an entire sequence of drawing exercises.

ASSIGNMENT

Draw a simple frame on the paper. The lines that describe this frame define the boundaries of the drawing. Adjust the frame as your view expands or contracts. Consider the plane of the paper synonymous with a wall that is punctured by a window. The entire window need not be visible within the frame—it may make for a more intriguing design to extend the window beyond the limits of the drawn frame.

A window frame provides a rectangular opening against which the measurement of objects within its view can be established. Derive the angles of the lines needed to represent recessional distance by comparing them to the rectangular frame of the window. Eye level should also be established relative to the frame of the window.

Make a rough geometric assessment of the multiplicity of shapes outside the window. Negative space will prove to be a valuable tool here. Create five small studies that are essentially linear. Hatch in two (at most three) significant dark shapes. Any medium or paper. No longer than 20 to 30 minutes.

Enlarge the best of these studies to approximately twice its original size and further develop it in any drawing medium. Continue the strategy of two or three important dark shapes, and add subordinate shapes of gray. Any medium or paper, as above. 1 hour.

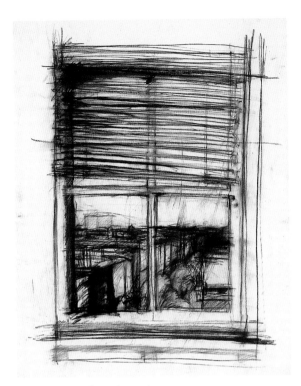

FIGURE 3 *top right*

The drawing plays with symmetry and framing. A pair of windows opens to view another pair of windows across a street or alley. The center line of the composition is the left edge of the center mullion in the foreground. The window in the left portion is centered; the identical window at the right is not. The use of tonal geometric shape reveals a highly readable pattern of light and shade that further emphasizes the different appearances of the two similar windows.

FIGURE 4 *bottom right*

A mate to figure 3, the drawing shows a window centered in the top portion of the composition. The inflected dark and light edges play against this centrality, as does the strong gesture of a dark tonal shape riding horizontally and upward toward the right of the page. An equally compelling movement is created by the bottom white negative shape stepping upward from left to right.

FIGURE 2 *left*

Two conditions of "looking through" are captured—looking through a window and looking through a window blind. The bottom two quadrants frame a geometrically summed-up vista of the low buildings of New York City's Lower East Side. Sunlight describes facades and the crowns of trees beginning to leaf. While light defines the closer view, a group of more distant buildings are massed in a rectangular dark shape with a dark strip reaching forward to identify the asphalt of an angled-in street. A dark vertical reaches up and threads into the slats of the window blind. The student's observant eye is apparent in the handling of the intervals between the slats. The vertical muntin, the window framing, and the blinds's pull-tapes are revealed and obscured.

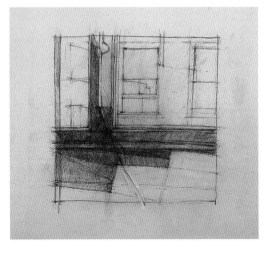

FIGURE 5

At first glance, the drawing appears to be a casual sketch. However, a clear architectonic structure lies just beneath its alluring skin, visible in the bold geometric shapes that divide the drawing in two. These basic shapes articulate all of the drawing's complex information. The lightly marked right half of the composition has its own surprising weight, while the leftward parade of parked cars is countered by the swan-necked gesture of a bent tree.

FIGURE 6

II. WINDOW: FOCUS

Focus is an essential tool to guide the eye in reading a spatially complex work. It targets the author's chief intention. Determine the focus of the depicted space. Is the focus the interior view of the wall, the window frame, the windowpane, or some distant point? Is it the slatted pattern of the half-drawn blind or the light pouring through certain windows across the street? Decide what strikes the eye, keeping in mind that while the eye's focus is akin to a camera's focus, it does not record information in the same way. Unlike a photograph, a drawing is made over a period of time, whether minutes or hours. The eye focuses and refocuses as the hand draws.

Hold a hand in front of the eyes, with fingers spread, and focus on something beyond. The fingers lose their detail and become shapes with soft edges, while the objects viewed between the fingers have sharply defined edges and distinct tonal contrasts. Use contrasting tonalities or vary the sharpness or softness of a line that describes an edge to further express an area of focus. Detail is another essential component of focus.

ASSIGNMENT

Draw four 30-minute studies within delineated frames—these studies may be in two pairs. Each of the pairs should frame the same view, but focus on the interior in one drawing and the exterior in the other drawing.

Using one of the four studies, complete a larger drawing. Use the paper itself as the frame, or inscribe a frame within the paper's parameters.

FIGURE 7

The major event occurs on the page's right side, where a gray shape to the right of the vertical sash joins the pair of water towers unexpectedly. The sharply delineated detail and rhythm of the small square windows emphasize the drama of focus. The beautifully and softly drawn top edge of a chair, which holds a garment, quietly attests to the interior space. A pull chord descending from a gathered window blind at the top also acknowledges the room. These interior discoveries, defined with minimal contrast, illustrate the difference between *subtlety* and *vagueness*.

FIGURE 8

The drawing is an example
of a more tonally modu-
lated focus, where the focus
itself is on the interior.
The bottom of the drawing
depicts a reading figure and
a plant, which are laced
together by the march of
vertical folds of a slightly
billowing curtain. The bare
window above frames the
facade across the street.
Note how the bays of
fenestration are rendered
in much lighter gray, putting
the distant plane in soft
focus.

FIGURE 9

Edges are softly delineated,
yielding an overall focus.
These devices affirm the
flatness of the right side
of the picture plane. At
the same time, the use
of perspective creates
the illusion of recessional
space on the left side of
the drawing. The vertical
center of the drawing is the
left edge of a wall parallel
to the picture plane; this
wall contains a vertical
course of windows, whose
shapes closely approximate
the proportions of the cars
on the street below. The
processional movement of
the cars toward a vanishing
point attests to a distance
that is impeded by the dark
wall at the street's dead
end. The similarity in scale
of the distant cars and the
nearby windows, coupled
with the overall lack of
focus, underscores the play
with spatial ambiguity.

III. WINDOW: TIME OF DAY

As light falls upon the object world, its effect can be translated in drawing into shapes of varying tones of gray. These shapes serve a double purpose. They allude to light, shadow, and local color. They also create a dark-and-light graphic pattern on the page, and this abstract pattern aids in organizing visual information. This portion of the window sequence brings the relevance of tone and shape into prominence, giving handwriting, hatching, and the clarity or softness of the line special attention.

ASSIGNMENT

Make three drawings of the same view through the same window, under three different lighting conditions—morning, afternoon, and night—or make use of the presence or absence of electric light. The frame of the view may be altered somewhat from drawing to drawing, but the same view should be maintained.

During the course of these studies, this same view will become a different assortment of shapes as the light changes. Shadows marry shapes to other shapes, often in unexpected ways, and light can either sharpen or bleach out their edges. Shadows may be hard or soft edged. Use any medium on any size paper. Draw within an inscribed frame. 1 hour for each drawing.

FIGURE 10

The glow from the lit windows of the Wanamaker Building contrasts brilliantly with the velvet black of the rubbed charcoal, a well-structured vision of the city at night. The drawing is a testament to keen observation, subtly rendering the difference in light and detail of each window. The work is an homage both to the drawings of Edward Hopper and Mies van der Rohe in the wholeness of its vision.

Figures 11 and 12 are renditions of the same view under different lighting conditions. The framing in each of the pair of drawings is similar but not identical, with distinct variations in the orchestration of shapes.

FIGURE 11 *top left*

Most prominent is the suspended, curved element that occupies the top center of the drawing. Appearing as a dark and heavy overhang, its large shape presses downward toward the floor plane.

FIGURE 12 *top right*

The angle of the light decreases the weight of the curved mass, which depicts its lit shape as if it were rising up through the top edge of the picture frame.

FIGURE 13 *left*

Three times of day are conflated and reconfigured in this Constructivist response. A square peephole window (most clearly delineated at the top, just left of the page's vertical center) reveals an angled skylight on the roof below. Portions of the skylight repeat across the page, illuminated from within or brightened by the sun. A rectangular patch of dark night sky at above left all but links at its bottom right corner to a dark interior wall in the center of the page, connecting their vast spatial distance. The bank of distant windows across the street repeats the square proportion of the peephole. The vents of the radiator covers, drawn in axonometric perspective at the bottom center and right of the page, echo the pattern of long rectangles of the skylight panes.

IV. WINDOW: REFLECTIONS

A compelling aspect of drawing windows at night is the windowpane itself. Due to the exterior darkness, the glass reflects the lit interior space; the windowpane becomes a mirror. At the same time, artificial light from the exterior world penetrates the reflection. One sees the surface of the glass and through the glass at the same moment.

ASSIGNMENT

Make three drawings from the same window. Draw one during daytime; the other two at night. In each of the night studies, address the reflections on the glass. Render reflections, like shadows, as shapes with hard or soft edges. All of the other considerations mentioned in the preceding window assignments should continue to be addressed here. Any drawing medium on any size paper, within an inscribed frame. I hour for each drawing.

FIGURE 14 *above*

FIGURE 15 *left*

The figure's elbow hinges to the chair just behind it in the backlit self-portrait. The dance of the traffic lights from the street below penetrates the subject's dark silhouette. Objects in the foreground indicate scale: the L-shaped metal plate and window lock (drawn in soft focus) measure the room's furniture and the street life caught in the reflection.

FIGURE 16 *right*

The drawing frames a dialogue between two window events. The left pane reflects a portrait of the artist at an easel; the right frames the street scene below. The half-raised blind—its left edge all but invisible—melds the left portion of the window into the plane of the page.

FIGURE 17 *left*

Reflections from the interior of the room merge with tree branches, a traffic light, and small figures from the street below. The mullions of the window frame, treated as negative space, join with a white rectangle, which represents the author's drawing pad. At the right the frame engages a portion of the author's body.

V. ROOM: TIME OF DAY

Between 1971 and 1974, when John Hejduk reinvented the interior spaces of the Foundation Building of The Cooper Union, he inserted a modernist building into a venerated brownstone container built by Peter Cooper in the mid-nineteenth century. In Hejduk's design, the journey of the eye is every bit as important as the movement of the body through the building. From tall thin openings and small square windows to the lines of columns in large open lobbies, the view is constantly reframed. Stepping back from the building's windows and focusing on framing views of the building's interior seemed a logical culmination to the Frame, Window, Room project.

Following Hejduk's example in this assignment, the element of visual surprise is particularly important. A foreground element might line up with something in the background; a shadow might hinge a chair to the floor, or the floor's reflective surface might make a column appear to pierce the floor.

ASSIGNMENT

Draw aspects of an interior under two different lighting conditions, possibly looking from one space into another, in which one space is dark and the other lit. Consider the parameters of the page as the frame. Any medium on any paper. 1 hour minimum.

Combine two different lighting conditions on the same page for the next drawing. Weave the two conditions together. The assignment presents new internal design demands: do not simply hinge a dark view to a light view. Give attention to the passageway through the drawing as the two conditions are woven together. This combination might give the drawing a Futurist or Cubist aspect. Any medium on any paper. 1 hour minimum.

FIGURE 18

FIGURE 19

An interior view of the third-floor lobby of the Foundation Building unfolds three times. The drawing moves from night at the left to morning at the right. The window wall casts its varied reflection on the polished floor. Reflections from another wall containing mirror-like elevator doors repeatedly intersect the floor. Columns appear and disappear into the ceiling and floor planes. Transparency and interpenetration abound. This image is an instance of Cubism translated from direct observation.

FIGURE 20

The drawing presents a vertical stacking of the spiral stair in the library under two different lighting conditions. The interpenetration of geometric shapes welds the drawing together. Note the rectangular chair back at bottom right that reappears at the center, with the spiral descent of the stair penetrating through it. There is a Constructivist interplay of positive and negative shapes.

The same hallway is the subject of these drawings. Cast shadows and reflected artificial light bounce along the surfaces of the corridor in figure 21 (above). The waves of light create a compelling gesture inviting the viewer's gaze inward toward the far wall lit by a large round reflected circle. Softness and transparency are the fabric of this nighttime view.

In figure 22 (left) the end of the corridor and the stairs, handrail, and distant door come sharply into focus. Daylight creates a bold rectangular pattern that falls on the stairs and the wall to the right. The bright natural light streams in through a square window across the corridor located beyond the page's parameters. In figure 21 the return of that window is represented by a dark vertical rectangle just to the left and above the stairs. The dark door in figure 22, its handle now in focus, is a compelling central element. In figure 21 the door is partly obscured by a circle of light.

SKULLS, HEADS, PORTRAITS

In my first drawing class I felt like I was surrounded by experts. It seemed that for some students, it was their second, third, or even fourth time taking drawing. I was convinced that they had been born with the ability to draw. Genetics had given them hands that could create masterpieces. When it came to drawing the model, my hand locked up. The model's face went from any ordinary face to something contorted, asymmetric, grotesque. Where did Professor Gussow find this guy? How could I compress this face into two dimensions? A half hour went by, and I had a crooked egg with an ear and a lot of erasure marks. As that first semester went on, the model started to look more human to me. By the second semester, he started to look human on my newsprint.

It took almost the two full semesters to realize that my hands were an extension of my eyes. It's been ten years, and my most difficult class has stuck with me. I draw on business cards at meetings, on receipts during rush hour, on paper tablecloths during meals, and for work everyday. My portraits are small and usually get thrown away or shoved into the glove compartment of my car, but they tie me to the people around me. For a minute or two, here and there, I engage in a quiet relationship with my subject. — ELIZA CHAIKIN

Physiognomy, the revelation of human character portrayed by facial features, is a study of endless fascination. In all manner of encounters in daily life, we study one another's faces to discern meaning. We do this naturally, without undue or even conscious consideration. In many of the arts—literature, theater, painting, drawing—the face and the play of its features is a matter of intense scrutiny. The features and their expressions are tools in an actor's trade; their configuration, the landscape for a portraitist's brush or pencil.

Attaining facial verisimilitude is an intense preoccupation for anyone invested in drawing the human form; achieving that likeness is keenly gratifying. Surprisingly, a major portion of the first semester of Freehand Drawing students are advised *not* to focus on likeness. In the rapid figure exercises (see the "Figure in Motion" studies, pp. 30–34), they are encouraged to ignore features altogether and simply to mark an abbreviated shape indicating the

FIGURE I

form of the head. (The jawline and the back of the skull might be accounted for, replacing the pervasive generic oval to show the head's spatial orientation.) Why divert the student's attention from this particularly compelling aspect of figure study? It is precisely because the desire for likeness is so spellbinding and appealing that once the focus is on the face the remainder of the body—its gesture, volume, occupation of space—will not receive appropriate attention.

Two weeks before Thanksgiving break, drawing from the skull and head exercises are introduced in studio. (At about the same time, students embark on studies from Giacometti, see pp. 66–69). In working from the skull, the focus is not on the skull alone; it is also on the skull in relation to the column of the spine and the spine's connection to the shoulder girdle (the encircling configuration of collarbones and shoulder blades), and their relationship to and independence from the ribcage. These relationships make up a critical and difficult territory in portraiture. How the head is held aloft is a spatial and structural configuration of particular interest to the student of architecture.

At Thanksgiving students have the occasion to draw family members, and it is important that a concern for structure underpin the desire for likeness.

Skulls and Heads

In no other portion of the body is the underlying bony structure so telling as it is in the head. The shape of the skull, the terrain of the face—made up by the prominence of the cheekbones and bridge of the nose, the depth of the eye sockets, the cut of the jaw—the set of the neck, the tilt of the shoulders, and the configuration of all of these together are as crucial to likeness as is the careful delineation of each facial feature.

EXERCISES

The Skull and Head exercises follow the pattern of those described in "The Figure and the Skeleton" (see pp. 51–54). Note that it is valuable to do a number of studies of the skull alone, rotating its position every 5 to 10 minutes. Do this exercise before posing the skeleton and model together to avoid focusing attention entirely on the model. Studies of the skull and model's head interposed are of particular value.

For the next 2½ hours, draw the skeleton positioned together with the two live models, with individual members of the class joining the posing group for 20- to 30-minute intervals. Each successive student takes a different place on the floor than the preceding student occupied. Students do not pose as an aggregate. Nonetheless, the resulting portrait group maintains its own spatial integrity and appears to be a group portrait. Easily mutable medium—charcoal, pastel, soft pencil—on any large horizontal paper 24" x 36" (or larger).

FIGURE 2

There is a clear-cut interposition of the skull and the model's head. The just-past-profile position of the model's head helps reveal the prominence of the cheekbone and the globe of the lidded eyeball set in its socket, with the eyebrow describing exactly the angularity of the socket's top ledge. A contour line indicates the location of the skull beneath the model's heavy mass of hair and the curve of the neck, allowing a visible forward thrust of the head.

Both the models' and skeleton's positions turn and stop at fixed intervals in a rotating arc in figures 3, 4, and 5.

FIGURE 3 *right*

Erasures made during the process of the drawing add dimensions of transparency and memory. The skull and model at the right overlap profile and three-quarter views, lending each image a curiously Cubist stamp. Although the head at right does not have a clearly marked underlying skull, its presence is implicit.

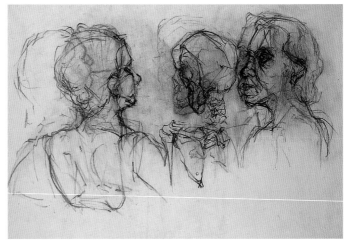

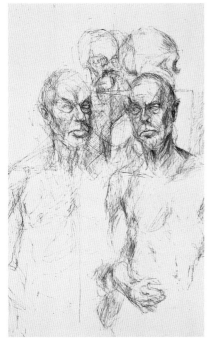

FIGURE 4 *left*

Two skulls are drawn just behind a double view of a male model. Finely modulated tones of pen and ink depict the three-quarter views, slightly inclined toward each other. While each face indicates its underlying skull, the drawing also presents a sensitive double portrait of the model as a specific human being. The work is enhanced by the gesture of the lightly sketched hand crossing his abdomen.

FIGURE 5 *right*

Students took turns posing. While minimal attention is given to the bony formations of the skeleton face, the portrayal of each individual classmate sharply reveals these structures. The clearly plotted-out volume of space occupied by each student gives rise to arresting spatial overlaps in the drawing. The arm of the standing figure on the far right shares a contour with the seated figure's collar, and his elbow penetrates that figure's chest. Such spatial ambiguities succeed in engaging and amazing the viewer's eye.

Portraits

Portraits are assigned four times over the course of the two semesters: a self-portrait is the first week's assignment; drawings of family members are requested during Thanksgiving break; and a self-portrait and a portrait of a classmate are assigned at the end of each semester. The self-portrait from the first week provides a benchmark for evaluation of growth, both artistic and psychological. The final portraits are a culmination and celebration of each individual's achievement.

ASSIGNMENTS

Family Portraits

Posing. Make sure your sitters are comfortable and engaged in some sedentary activity—watching TV, reading, board games, cards, even sleeping—distracting them from the self-consciousness of being drawn. Include some portion of the body beyond head, neck, and shoulders. Body language and shape are as telling of likeness as facial features are; one recognizes friends, even mere acquaintances, halfway down the street by these characteristics.

Likeness. While it is not possible altogether to dismiss the desire for likeness, avoid, as much as possible, aiming for it. Throughout the drawing process, keep previously acquired drawing concepts—placement on the page, the gesture of the sitter, the angle of the neck, the set of the shoulders, the sculpture of the entire head, the planar landscape of the face in which the features are discovered—foremost in your thoughts. Always seek the skull beneath the skin. Likeness enters through the side door, most often when other aspects of drawing are at the forefront of attention. Note: Family members and friends are likely to point to discrepancies between their view of themselves and the image you are drawing. Do not feel impelled to please. Never alter your drawing to accommodate your sitter. This is good practice in the long run—and character building. Any medium, paper, and paper size. Any serious amount of time, as this will vary with the patience of your sitter.

Self Portrait and Portrait of a Classmate. Depict at least three quarters of the body in one of the two drawings.

In the self-portrait consider the gestures you make while drawing as an essential element within the work. Use mirrors to activate the space in an unexpected way. When drawing the self-portrait—if it is the three-quarter-body drawing—consider touching the mirror with some portion of your body to open the space of the page outward to the space in front of the picture plane.

In drawing a bust portrait—head, neck, shoulders—locate the head securely on the stem of the neck. Notice the manner in which the neck emerges from the shoulders. The neck is always columnar in form. Do not treat it merely as two lines stuck on under the jaw. In a portrait the set of neck and shoulders is critical to lending gesture to the drawing.

While all features are essential to the facial landscape, eyes are usually the most compelling—engaging the viewer's own gaze or looking distinctly away from it. This engagement or nonengagement lends a psychological gesture to the work. Remember that the eye is not a flat lozenge or almond-shaped feature ending at the edge of the lids. Always search for the globe of the eye, and draw it in the depth of the socket in which it is set. Any medium. Large paper is recommended. 1 hour at minimum.

With the participation of family members, students reveal candid scenes in figures 6 and 7.

FIGURE 6 *right*

The couple is aware of being studied, but the drawing portrays them lounging with their attention fixed elsewhere, unmindful of their role. The volumes of their torsos and limbs press into the mattress and bedclothing, revealing body shape and language. Their barely defined features express the skulls' influence on structure. Nonetheless, characteristic gesture (note the woman's curled-under toes) and the clear sculpture of facial planes acknowledge likeness. A thin dark shape, beginning as a shadow cast by the bedclothes, ropes around the woman's limbs and lashes onto the elbow of the man, creating a passageway through the drawing.

FIGURE 7 *left*

Head, body, and bedclothes nestle snugly against the bottom of the page. The curves of the bedding encase the body of the sleeping woman and leave her face as the focus; her features are assuredly carved in strong dark and light contrast—this planar modeling exists only in the face. Three deeply incised lines proceed outward from the mask of the face and hold it—like a faceted stone held in a setting.

Examination of the gestures the body assumes while making a self-portrait occurs in figures 8 and 9. The head-on approach confronts the self and the viewer. In each the large drawing pad is placed horizontally while the mirror's plane is vertical. The student must rely more on memory to reproduce her body posture and head position. (Her view of herself in the vertical mirror is no longer available as she bends her head in order to draw. Typically, both pad and mirror are vertical, and the drawer's eye can scan subject and paper all-but-simultaneously.) Note that apart from blind-contour drawing, all drawing from observation utilizes some degree of visual memorizing.

FIGURE 8

Foreshortening conflates shoulders, chest, and hips into the top span of an arch in this self-portrait. The head, centered on this span, confronts the viewer. The axis of the head, echoed by the angle of the drawing arm, countered by the bent arm, hand on knee, all combine to heighten the figure's animation.

FIGURE 9

In this drawing the student leans so far forward that her face seems to press against the picture plane as though it were a sheet of glass. Her features emerge through the dark tones that result from backlighting, challenging the viewer to discover them. Strongly contrasting tones of shadow and light reveal the volumes of the body and also provide a striking patterning by which the drawing may be read abstractly.

Two students take on the issue of extending the picture plane into the space in front of it by touching the mirror with one hand in figures 10 and 11.

FIGURE 10 *left*

The overlapped positions of the hand engaged in the drawing process further animate the drawing. The nude upper torso adds a dimension of intimacy—even voyeurism—to the act of self-portraiture.

FIGURE 11 *below*

Lighting and framing provide a theatrical setting for two self-portraits. The back-to-back postures and the thrust of the arms suggest an artistic duel. The arm and hand touching the mirror acts as a vector, directing the viewer's eye into the more distant center of the drawing. Here the author has played on duality by setting his self-portrait in the background within a receding series of darkened planes. The foreground contains the mirrored image of a classmate, his reflection set in light.

FIGURE 12

While the head is the central focus in the drawing, a cupped hand is included in the composition. The overlay of the fingers, drawn twice, lends the hand a subtle motion. The student presents herself, head in a turban, turned slightly away, eyes gazing back out—an homage to Vermeer; a young woman, lips barely parted—as if about to speak. The drawing tells of the next moment, and of time.

FIGURE 13

The Cubist push and pull of the planes of the face achieves animation. A diagonal seam cuts through the drawing, descending from the part in the hair, down through the forehead, along the left edge of the nose, cutting under to the indentation of the upper lip, and picking up underneath the sleeve. This diagonal seam enforces the tilted axis of the head, supported by the counter thrust of the neck and shoulders. The assured calligraphy of the tousled hair reveals the skull beneath.

FIGURE 14 *far left*

FIGURE 15

The gaze of the figure focuses strongly outward. The neck, entering from the bottom edge, together with the lines emanating in radial fashion from the skull, suggests a recent thrust upward into the space of the page. The boldly contrasting tones of planar modeling, the assertive handwriting, and the large scale of the head relative to the size of the page all speak of purposeful assurance.

TREES

Trees surround us. They hold us captive to their season.... Trees celebrate life and death. Their branches flare upward in the sky, attempting to offer perches to angels, and trees root down into the earth encompassing the remains of the long dead. — JOHN HEJDUK, *Tree*

The botanist Colin Tudge gives a definition of a tree that a child might give: "a big plant with a stick up the middle."[1] Summing up some sixty thousand known species, this is a splendidly generic definition. It is entirely consonant with the manner in which most children will draw a tree—a large green lollipop atop its vertical stick. Such a pictogram harks back to the pea-pod drawings done from memory on the first day of Freehand Drawing. It also brings to mind the tree represented as a bundle of twigs, pervasive in architectural representation, and the deckle-edged circle with its center dot that is a standard icon for the tree-in-plan drawings. Such a convention is a convenient visual logo, but it does not enhance the architect's

individual imprimatur. Tudge's further remarks are salutary, aiding the student of architecture in turning away from such conventions. He comments on the tree as "one of the wonders of the universe...remarkably complex...minutely structured...and infinitely various."[2] A compelling argument for the necessity and delight of observation.

Chief among the reasons that tree drawing is the final studio project of Freehand Drawing is simply that it is spring! There is new bright light and longer daylight hours; armed with a rack of folding chairs, drawing supplies, and models, the class marches to a small park just south of the Foundation Building. The park's triangular plan is edged with an iron fence and perhaps a dozen trees. Mid-April is a good time to study trees—while they are still fairly bony and just beginning to show new life.

The academic year began with the pea pod, an object easily held both in memory and the hand. It is appropriate to stretch the skills and concepts acquired over the course of the two semesters by concluding with the tree—a form of such contrasting scale and complexity. Drawing it requires both observation of the particular and the ability to make larger abstractions to cope with the many branches, the multiplicity of twigs, the myriad leaves, and the complex irregularities of the bark that embraces the girth of the tree.

The interchangeable language often used to describe trees and human bodies—trunk, limbs, crown—adds a dimension of metaphor to the endeavor. Models (now clothed, of course) sometimes join the scene—leaning against the tree or seated at its base—to enforce the reference to the body and to add the dimension of scale. Drawing from the tree brings forward and challenges the concepts developed over the many weeks of drawing from the figure—those of volume, gesture, and the interpenetration of form and space. Further, the acquired editing

FIGURE 3

skills—necessary, given the impossibility of rendering each branch, twig, and leaf—generate a new freedom to invent a handwriting that will abbreviate and abstract. While lopping off a limb or placing one in an inexact position is quite noticeable and disconcerting in representing the figure, a tree drawing is entirely forgiving of such indiscretions. The whole is decidedly greater than the sum of its parts, yet the parts demand attention.

ASSIGNMENTS

Although the studio moves outdoors to study trees, the following preparatory and adjunct assignments aid in confronting the actual tree. While the human body is an invaluable metaphor in comprehending the tree's gestalt and the jointed aspect of its limbs, the tree's larger-than-life scale is daunting.

Master Studies of Trees. Examples of drawings of trees can be found in the work of the following artists—Leonardo, Titian, Dürer, Bosch, Bruegel, Rubens, van Dyck, Rembrandt, Lorrain, Ruisdael, Corot, van Gogh, Cézanne, and Mondrian. Look for reproductions where the handwriting is clear and comprehensible. For the following studies, refer back to methods described in the first semester's master studies (see pp. 55–58).

In the first week or two of Master Tree Studies, draw only portions of the tree—draw the trunk alone, a portion of the trunk with some limbs emerging, then a portion of the trunk moving into the root system. Note that the limbs and roots do not join abruptly to the trunk like pieces of plumbing; they evolve from its mass in a gradual fashion. Draw each portion rapidly and repeatedly. Sharpened charcoal pencil, carbon pencil, pencil, or pen on any size white paper. ½ hour.

Entire-tree Study. Notice the tree's gesture—whether leaning, upright, twisting. Take note of its proportions. What proportion is the mass of its leaves compared to its trunk? Again, draw rapidly. Do not be concerned with likeness, but rather with "live-ness." Same materials as above. ½ hour.

During the second and third weeks, paralleling the season's change and the budding and subsequent leafing of the bare branches, make studies of leaf "handwriting." Examine the abstracting notations the masters have employed to sum up the mass and volume of the tree's crown. Attempt a range of handwriting, drawing rapidly from one or several of the artists listed above. Use whatever medium seems fitting for all of the above studies—pencil, pen, ink wash, charcoal pencil, charcoal on any paper. ½ hour.

EXERCISES

WEEKS I–II

At this point in the semester, the mostly bare branches reveal the tree's structure. Begin with rapid studies of portions of the actual tree—to resonate with studies from masters described above. Develop a handwriting that discusses the girth of the tree—not merely its outline or the texture of its bark. Varying with the species, the lines made by the bark's texture may suggest a handwriting that describes the tree's circumference. Again, it is best to draw this rapidly—not slavishly. Any medium on any paper. 30 minutes to 1 hour.

A negative-space study of the trunk's moving into limbs and branches is an excellent way to discover the varied intricacies of patterning they create. This aids in avoiding generic spacing (where all negative space intervals are drawn at more or less the same size due to visual inattention). Any medium on any paper. 1 hour.

Draw a study of the entire tree. The model may be included in the scene, leaning against the tree or seated nearby. Incorporate classmates and other figures as desired. Note that the figure is a measure of the tree. Avoid the tendency to make the figure too large; the figure is no longer the star of the page but an element in the whole of the compositional structure. Any medium on any paper 24" x 36" or larger. 2 hours or longer.

WEEKS III–IV

Apply what has been learned from drawing foliage from master studies to drawing from direct observation of actual trees. The trees have begun to leaf and some are already in full foliage by this time. Show the massing of leaves in relation to the branches supporting them. Do this rapidly and repeatedly. Any media. Any paper. 20 to 30 minutes.

When mapping out the page, also include lines that indicate buildings, figures, and vehicles that appear in the spaces between the trunks, branches, and masses of leaves. Draw a quick underdrawing of the tree(s) first, then lightly mark in blocks of shape that will be the basis for buildings, fences, vehicles, etc. Establish your eye level early so that you will have a consistent perspectival reference throughout the drawing process.

Focus and negative space are critical issues. If the focus is the tree(s) in foreground or middle ground, minimize architectural notations or eliminate them altogether using geometric blocks of negative space. Use architectural detail judiciously as a counterpoint to the trees. Reduce the repetition of banks of windows to negative spaces when appropriate. When windows are attended to in detail, differentiate them so that each one is distinct. In drawing visually dense situations, negative space is an essential design ally. Areas left lightly marked or entirely blank serve as welcome visual oases. Any medium on any paper. 2½ to 3 hours.

Exploration of the hierarchy of trunk, limb, and branch is the primary theme in figures 4, 5, and 6.

FIGURE 4 *left*

The drawing meticulously examines the evolution of the major limbs pulling and stretching upward and outward from the poised yet twisting trunk. The drawing displays its own hierarchy of values, focusing on a midsection of the trunk. The language of dense handwriting investigates the complexities of the trunk's column, and the protuberances of knots and cut-off limbs are articulated with attention but still manage to keep their place in a well-orchestrated whole. The giraffe-neck shape of the upper trunk arches to the right of the page while another major limb curves backward, its smaller branches grasping at the left half of the page. The drawing emanates from the darkened region of the trunk, as the more lightly drawn, lesser branches and twigs observe each bend, articulation, and crossover.

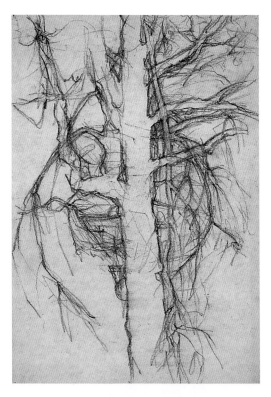

FIGURE 5 *right*

The centrally placed trunk assumes an all-but-ghostly presence in the negative space study of the intervals of the crossing limbs and branches. There is a remarkable flip between flatness and volume: volume is suggested by a very faint tracery that indicates markings on the bark encircling the trunk. In addition a light underlay of lines investigates the movement of branches surrounding the trunk, giving the impression of their vibration. Flatness is achieved by the equally inflected dark contours that emphasize the puncture of spaces between the branches.

FIGURE 6

The drawing addresses the issue of scale. A foreground group of rounded trees share a rightward gesture, countered by the shared leftward motion of several lightly contoured trees in the distance. The page boasts a strikingly architectonic composition. The right edge of the most centrally located tree forms the boundary of the foreground grouping while its left edge serves as framing for the right-hand stand of trees. Each edge of the tree serves as a parameter for the different groupings, creating an ambiguous spatial overlap between the two vertical portions of the composition.

The urban setting assumes a role in figures 7 and 8.

FIGURE 7 *facing page*

In the foreground the trunk of a tree is cut by the left edge of the page. The tree in its entirety is located in front of the picture plane. The strong carving of its protuberances (where limbs were severed) suggests a coat of armor as the tree appears to stand guardian to the side of the path that curves into the park from the right foreground. Along the path the more distant trees stand in dancelike postures. The trees' skeletal branches transparently suspend planar slices, described by a network of lighter lines. They indicate the massing of leaves that will sprout from the many budding branches. Caught in this transparent scrim of lines, an orthogonal block of buildings defines the park's parameters.

FIGURE 8 *above*

A path again introduces us to a small city park. The avenue of trees at center leads to a background wall of buildings that edge the park. Windows, roughly marked to indicate perspective, also serve to differentiate one building from another. These windows peek through branches that boast an array of light-to-dark clumps of charcoal hatching, simple groups of marks that successfully depict the massing of leaves and the penetration of the afternoon light. The light edges the columns of the tree trunks and cuts brighter slices across the dark area of the entering path.

Figures 9 and 10 each make advantageous use of negative space and focus.

FIGURE 9 *facing page*

This quiet drawing reveals an artist's process—it is a study arrested at a certain stage of its evolution. Two trees rise from a mound, bounded by an embankment. The trunks are well developed, the emergence of their limbs and branches precisely articulated. The background lightly threads in a few buildings. Cars move or are parked in the middle ground. Dark lines that weave the brush in the center and the tree at the right hold one car in the foreground. Two more-distant cars, faintly marked and minimally detailed, merge with the whispered notations of the buildings beyond.

FIGURE 10 *above*

The area where major branches of the two center trees cross and form an arch is the compelling focus of this work. A darkened vertical line makes a seam between the adjacent buildings and bisects the arch. This seam divides the page into a positive and a negative portion: to the left is explicit detail—figures, fire escape, carefully differentiated windows—to the right, the faintest measuring lines. This oasis of space serves to buffer the strong diagonal thrust of the right-hand tree.

PART II

DIRTY DRAWING
ADVANCED PROJECTS

Having explored the fundamental vocabulary of freehand drawing in first year, students develop drawings based on themes of their own choosing in the Advanced Drawing Seminar, which meets weekly for extensive group and individual critiques. A number of questions might be posed: How are these freely chosen themes relevant to the education of an architect? What is the value in drawing the surge forward of jockeys on horseback, the body's ritual movements in throwing a pot, the bravura gestures of a pianist's arms and hands at work, the fixed location of pastured cows? How would tracking these images develop an architect's spatial vocabulary?

The study of the other arts—literature, poetry, film, dance—is important in expanding the architect's mind and vision. But all too often, if an advanced drawing course is in an architecture-school curriculum, it is held captive to utility. It is likely to be viewed either as a means of representation of "built" projects or as a "hobby" class—draw the model for 20 minutes, take a break, turn the page, draw the model again.

Imagination lies in the realm of memory and dreams, deeply rooted in the facts, forms, events, and spaces of our actual lives. Flights of fancy take off from that which can be touched, tasted, measured, and observed. All memory is set in past or recent circumstance. We dream in images, as Friedrich Nietzsche proposed in *The Birth of Tragedy* (1867). These images have locations—rooms, streets, bridges, oceans. However, the development of a project that ranges from the observable to the realm of imagination requires a certain level of technical proficiency, a grasp of the basic concepts of drawing.

FIGURES 1 AND 2

right and facing page

Taku Shimizu, studies of hands derived from Leonardo da Vinci, Last Supper, 1498. Charcoal on newsprint. The surface of the paper acts as a kind of foil on which the gestural movements of the hands are projected and superimposed. The process of distilling ("drawing") the hands from the context begins to alter the spatial relationship between the apostles, and by extension, re-establishes extents of the space.

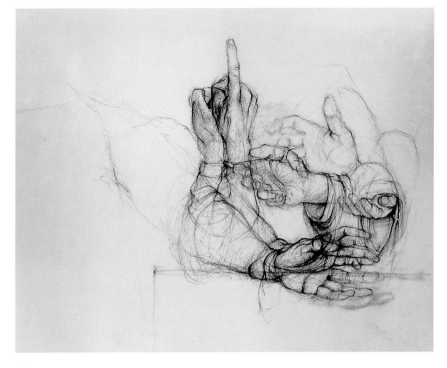

The "dirt" in the above heading refers to the fallout from charcoal, pencil, pastel, pen, and ink wash; it is the fingerprints, smudges, erasures, spatters, and drips of wash. It derives from the repetitive process of searching through drawing, of sifting through layers to find the gold—the essential element. The struggle to conquer a particular medium is only a part of the endeavor—it is the struggle to find resonance between the visual world as it engages our eye and the realm of our imaginings.

Although dirty drawing is at the other end of the graphic spectrum from what might be achieved in drafting with an instrument-aided, finely pointed 9H pencil or the unvarying line generated on a computer, the drawings of the free hand serve to inform the mind and hand that employ these tools—tools indeed imperative to professional practice. The truly free hand makes investigations that to some appear messy but that have their own aesthetic quality. These drawings serve to clarify the direction of the next step and simultaneously clarify (or even reformulate) the meaning and intent of the theme.

At this level of drawing education, the student learns to create drawings that incorporate themes that have grown in the crucible of each individual imagination, thought, and experience. Like the process of creative writing in which the author writes and rewrites again and again, the drawing process goes beyond merely correcting or expunging lines or tonalities that seemed tentatively or clumsily embraced in the first study. It simultaneously leads to rethinking and clarifying the direction of the intended work itself. In working toward that goal, the development of technique will simultaneously be honed.

GUILTY PLEASURE

NINA HOFER

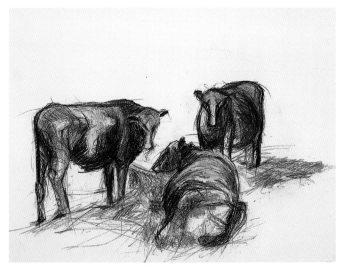

FIGURES **3** AND **4**

Charcoal and gesso on paper

The Cows began in the guilty pleasure of weekends during which I fled school and city for a farm owned by friends. Made in a state of curiosity and play, the drawings were more potent than other things made heroically with effort and anxiety. Architecture schools tend to use time in a very specific way, mining the power of the charette and the deadline. Life (and "practice") has other keys; learning occurs in varied temporal modes.

Advanced Drawing harvested the power of the ritual. Significance accrues too in the practice of a daily task through the layering of parallel experiences and loosely connected thoughts. Interstitial time allows for the transformative application of unconscious thought, creating moments of unexpected revelation. The synthetic nature of the backward glance and the organizing character of the collection encourage synchronicities. Projects take on generative power as a body of work begins to talk to itself.

Some of the most open-ended exploration at The Cooper Union took place in the space between the rigor of the very public design studio and Sue Gussow's carefully constructed and more private precinct of investigation. Our drawing probes had a decisive effect on our thesis work and on our subsequent development as designers.

The cow drawings gathered to themselves a coming to terms with an unstylized and weighty feminine, the myth of the virgin, the liminality of the gate, and a probing of the nested space of the gravid. I rediscover them from time to time, although they are certainly a project of settling into self, and not of later stages in life.

FIGURE 5

Charcoal and gesso on paper

GAUDÍ'S PHOTOGRAPHS

YEON WHA HONG

In my thesis year, while I was researching in the library, I came across a book of architect Antoni Gaudí's sculptural work—specifically, photographic studies for his sculptures for the Sagrada Família Cathedral. He used his employees as models for various traditional religious sculptures: stonemasons as models for Christ, women for Madonna and Child, heralding angels, and so on. He had them pose between two angled mirrors to produce a 360-degree view of the figure.

I drew for the rest of the semester from small photocopies of these photographs. I was intrigued by the space of that mirror-contraption—its depth and flatness and the varieties of spaces it created. As the original figure is multiplied and visually flattened, other figures emerge as shadows and patterns, occurring first on the planes of the mirrors, then in the photographs, then in the photocopies I was drawing from.

Freehand drawing teaches one to observe with the eye, to see with the hand, and also to see what is not necessarily there, but could be inferred. How I draw informs how I design—not only in the sense that it enables me to see well, but also to explore things that I want to see. Being trained to draw—to frame, to compose, to observe and invent—is, in short, being trained in how to make sense of the world.

URBAN INTIMACY: THE MANICURE

MAYA MAXWELL

FIGURE **6**

Gesso and charcoal pencil
on paper

FIGURE **7**

Pencil on paper

The desire to take on the subject of manicures stemmed from visual and contextual reasons. The spatial qualities of the manicure process are compelling—the space between two people, the aggressive and gentle movement of the hands performing the task, and the passivity and malleability of the recipient's hands. The anonymous, mechanical nature of the black apron (worn by the manicurist) is a backdrop for the false intimacy of hands being massaged and conditioned, the nails painted. In this room there is an incredible juxtaposition of intimacy and alienation, of nurturing in exchange for currency.

Many factors came into play during the production of the work. I wanted to retain the energy of the place and experience while working from photographs in a studio. In order to avoid the rigidity of emulating a single frozen image and a predetermined composition, multiple photographs were printed and displayed. Different scales and mediums were attempted. Some of the works explored a quiet precision while others focused on gestural energy. The question of narrative came up: To what extent is context necessary, and at what point does context become narrative? To what extent is narrative a legitimate element in drawing and when is it illustrative? The interest for me lay in the search—rigor of process, the energy of experimentation, and the memory of experience—not in one answer. The strongest drawings retained all of these elements, but revealed none. They existed autonomously.

FROM WHALES
TO COAL MINES

DANIEL MERIDOR

The story of the Svalbard archipelago in the Arctic Ocean is a story of exploitation. Its status as a no-man's-land, or *terra nullius*, a national status widely agreed upon since the seventeenth century, allowed for the misuse of its natural resources without restrictions and taxation. While ships competed for whales to hunt at sea, mining companies vied for coal with the erection of new structures on land. They assumed that conquering more territory would strengthen their case in future negotiations for national status of the archipelago. After World War II, only Norwegian and Russian settlements survived on Svalbard, while coal mines owned by other nationalities were abandoned.

Today, old conveyor belts stretch throughout the island into the port. Deserted towers, houses, and mines still stand as a reminder of a different era. These structures struggle under the loads of snow, water, rust, and time.

In this series of drawings, I reincarnated these structures by reconstructing them over the landscape. The first act was careful observation of the new qualities of decay the structures had acquired by being exposed to large amounts of water over time—qualities that did not appear in their construction drawings and would be less present if the structures were active and inhabited.

Then I drew a series of precise architectural ink drawings, which revealed portions of these structures in different scales. These drawings were soaked in water, left to dry, and redrawn over and over again as a Sisyphean task. The process allowed the memory of the original proposal for these structures to fade and established a new structural terminology—broken, detached, additive, compressed, and tensioned—used to articulate the new construction.

Water, then, became the main motif of the project—from the actual destruction of these structures to the fading memory of their origin. Ultimately it provoked a reconstruction of the existing above the jagged ground of Svalbard.

DRAWING SWIMMING

AMBER CHAPIN

Seated figures, self-portraits, glasses, and bowls—the objects and people that surround me—are the subject of this series. The intimacy of scale and simplicity of the series allowed me to focus both on the medium, line, and color, and on the depth of my relation to its subjects. For instance, I often drew a musician who could sit for hours perfectly still but intensely, almost painfully focused, thinking—I assume—of music. How does one draw a portrait with no overt movement but fraught with nervous energy? The hidden and unrecognized crept into the drawings. I find them, despite their playful lines, grim and skeletal. They have for me some of the anxiety of their time, fall 2001.

Over time the drawings became progressively smaller and remarkably dense. Someone in class gave me a masking fluid—a transparent, fast-drying, impermeable medium. Drawing with the mask on a white piece of paper, I could not see the mask as I drew, because it was transparent. I had to remember what I had laid down. Only as I began to draw over the mask in color did its lines and shapes appear as a ghosted white underlayer. There was always a slippage between the mask and the color overdrawing, between what I remembered having drawn in mask and what was revealed on the page. The figure in color would appear slightly in front of or behind the figure in mask while still being ostensibly the same figure.

This slippage helped me learn to draw through and into objects. The joint of a wrist might have some resonance with the spindle of the leg of a chair. Even when I could not actually see the spindle because it was blocked from view by the leg of the figure, it would get pulled into the drawing—seen through, or on top of, or instead of the figure's leg.

The closest likeness to this experience of drawing is the space you sometimes discover when swimming. The sun comes through the water above; you feel it across your neck and back and legs. The light makes undulating patterns of dark and incredibly bright light on the sand below, which itself is shifting. Murky organisms' spines, the fingers of vegetation waver. Your shadow is a dark broad shape stealing across of all this. But it too is transparent. The medium of the experience is the warmth or cool, the evanescence and whimsy of water.

FIGURE 10

Watercolor and liquid frisket (mask) on paper

FIGURE II

Oil bar and paint on particle board

FULTON FISH MARKET: FROZEN MOTION

GIA MAINIERO

I grew up down the block from the Fulton Fish Market. The market itself was always an enigma to me, knowing nothing more of it than the beeping of trucks parking late at night, the bright lights at the end of the block, the shiny slick on the streets, and the smell that lingered throughout the day.

When the market's closing was announced, I decided to visit on an early morning to see up close my mysterious long-term neighbors. Expecting to be more interested in the activity of the market and bustle of the sales, I was surprised to find myself completely absorbed by the fish themselves— how alive they looked, frozen in position as if still in midswim, eyes staring back up at me. The bright colors of their skin against the silvery ice and rusty steel bins gave a mystical feel to the bare fluorescent-lit market building. They didn't seem dead but simply frozen in a sort of limbo between the sea and their final fate in a New York restaurant.

As I set out to capture this in my paintings, I became interested in both the table that these creatures rested on—the consistent horizon—and the ice in which they were nestled—the substance that broke this line and suspended them again, as if still in water. The ice became an adventure of its own—how to depict a material with no form besides that of the creatures buried under it, and with no color other than the reflections of the fish's metallic skin. In the paintings, it served as both a cradle for the fish, to reveal certain parts of their bodies, and to allow others to sink below and disappear. The ice also became a field of negative space on the page, allowing the painting to also surface and submerge.

THE PIANIST

LIS CENA

The exploration of the potentials of the hand as a tool of expression, in a world unbound by the framework of parallel and perpendicular precision, was new territory for me. Discovering these potentials and appropriating them through the art of mark-making gave shape to this project.

Viewing the hands as structures that move, express, create, provided an essential dimension through which the hand as a part of the whole—the body—could be observed and understood. It is through interactions and relationships to other structures that hands become the artist-in-making. This awakened my desire to explore the art of the pianist. The piano, as a construct of precise structures within a rigid frame of endless possibilities of tone and color, is a potent and fertile ground for the exploration of the hand as a construct of natural expression, characterized by its freedom of movement.

After learning to draw the hand as a form with its inherent articulation, I produced a series of sketches of a pianist in the act of playing. I observed that hands were no longer hermetic movable structures. They are endings that derive their expression from the body and are informed by the mind and the spirit. The two drawings engage this investigation—an expression of these very qualities of the hands as parts of the body and the depiction of their movements, interactions, and expressions as essential qualities in the process of music-making.

The lessons that have come from investigating the hands through drawing have added to my understanding of drawing as an artistic, poetic, and intellectual practice. They have also informed my understanding of the art of the piano. Only when one learns the hand's capacities can one can master thought.

FIGURES 12 AND 13

Charcoal and charcoal
pencil on paper

FIGURE 14

Graphite and collaged
colored paper

SURREAL ABSTRACTION

PAUL DALLAS

This project originated from several key sources. The first is the work of the Armenian American artist Arshile Gorky. Completed in the time between the end of Surrealism and the rise of Abstract Expressionism, Gorky's paintings are highly imaginative hybrids. The second source for the project is the city itself. I have lived in New York since June 2001, and my architectural education and experience of the city have been colored as much by the landscape of disaster as by the landscape of recovery. Now that we are also embroiled in a war, the fear of impending violence has become forever linked in my mind to the urban condition.

These drawings evoke an interior land scape—a place between dream and awakening—filled with unease. An invented vocabulary of shape and form inhabit the stagelike space of the page. The chosen biomorphic forms are formally alluring and open up the possibility for wildly different associations.

Above all, they hold a strange familiarity that references living forms at many different scales.

At first I worked loosely, incorporating automatic writing techniques for form-finding and developing "all-over" compositions. Later I created highly charged scenes composed of fewer elements. These pieces describe tense interactions between several biomorphic "characters." One formal device that remained constant was the elimination of a ground plane—the characters hover ambiguously within the frame of the page. While the imagery has a sinister edge, there is a great deal of humor that can be found underneath.

The medium of powdered graphite was ideal, creating atmospheric space that emphasized texture and edge. I chose to work primarily in black and white; color was used sparingly to create visual impact and to counterpoint the soft smoky grays and thick blacks of graphite. Unlike the black and white forms, which were sculpted out of graphite, the collaged color forms were literally cut out and thus have different physicality.

FIGURE/FABRIC/ FURNITURE

DAVID WEILAND

One of my objectives in drawing is the faithful depiction of what is seen. In the beginning, this was almost all I could do—just look and try to get it right. My project has dealt with different aspects of portraiture, and realism was the initial vehicle for expressing the nature of the subject. However, in struggling to break from a method based primarily on observation, I began to construct increasingly imagined settings and characters. My interest in realism did not disappear, but became critical as a support for what was imagined.

My focus turned to the clothing and furniture surrounding the body and how they could physically and visually influence the portraits. The drawing no longer follows a single visual logic. Different components of the setting may belong to different characters and are, in some sense, created by them. The mutable environment became an extension of the body—a body language—and thus a form of communication between the mute characters.

The construction of a meaningful continuum between body, clothing, upholstery, and furniture is fundamentally an architectural problem. Bridging the gap between ourselves and the built environment needs a language in which material is free to behave as humans do.

FIGURES 15 AND 16

Pencil on paper

THE RACE

LAUREN ZUCKER

Within the confines of ten furlongs, there are metacorporeal aspects of the horse race never experienced by the spectator. I first experienced the horse race through the medium of literature. Each moment of the race was decompressed, and the experience was unfolded. Drawn out in detail were the visceral relationships between horse and jockey, the operations and politics implicit in a racing farm, the strategies and traditions of breeding and training, the excitement of race-day mornings, and the intent behind every move during the course of the race. The race compresses the life experience of each racer—horse or jockey—into two minutes.

Through drawing I fold the life narrative of the racer into gesture; then, as in the race,

montage the narratives of different racers. I found inspiration for expressing this agony of entanglement in Picasso's *Guernica* (1937). The narrative gesture of war is not unlike that of the horse race.

There is a dichotomy in horse racing that at once evokes both nobility and grit. I found this to exist even at the scale of the horse's eye, loaded with noble courage and animalistic fear—and in the relationship between the fear in the horse's eye and the focused determination of the jockey's eye.

The process of these drawings was subtractive, many beginning as a coat of black oil bar. The slow drying time of oil bar and linseed oil gave me the time to carve the horses' bodies into the blackness. I reworked portions of the drawing repeatedly, conveying motion and time lapse through the multiplicity of elements, such as the doubling of the jockey's hand in different positions.

FIGURE 17

Oil bar and linseed oil on paper

Ink on paper

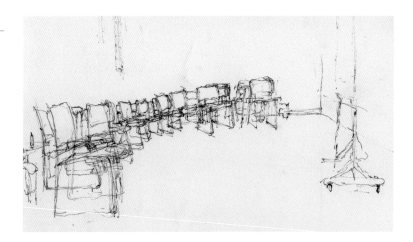

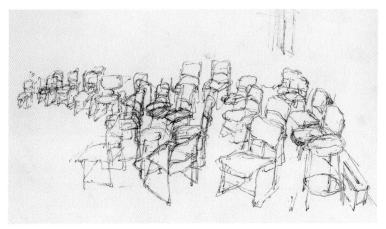

PORTRAIT OF A ROOM

JOSE A. ORTEZ

Room 312, the subject of these drawings, is a multipurpose classroom in the third floor of the Foundation Building at The Cooper Union whose character transformed as the activities within it changed. I wondered whether the room could have its own personality. Through the drawings I discovered secrets about the room and the nature of the life it could house.

In the process of capturing the essence of these changes, I became fascinated with the chairs that occupied the room because they were never in the same position twice. Their changing configurations were a record of the activities that had previously taken place there. By reading their positions in the space in relation to one another, the chairs told the story of the room—revealing where the professors had been sitting, the kind of class that had been held, and sometimes how many people had attended the class. After three months of observing the room I discovered a direct relationship between drawing a space and understanding its history.

GRANDFATHER STUDIES

DANIEL WEBRE

My grandfather drawings arose out of a what-to-draw crisis. I was completely stuck, and it hadn't occurred to me that it wasn't necessary to think of an original or unusual subject. A classmate remembered that I had drawn my grandfather as part of a first-year assignment and suggested that I find a subject with the same immediacy. The simple act of portraiture is direct and uncomplicated and freed me to explore questions of space.

I discovered something about photography and portraiture in the process. When I began this series of drawings, they were from photographs I had taken of my grandfather sitting in the chair he always uses. I felt compelled to include many details from the photos that were not crucial. After a few weeks, I abandoned this process altogether and drew him from memory. The space was reduced to as few elements as possible, elements that became characters that I would play with—space, body, and chair.

FIGURES 20 AND 21

Charcoal over gesso base on paper

THE OCEAN

BETH MILLER

The ocean studies originated on the coast of Fire Island, an island off the southern shore of Long Island, near my family's home. I was initially drawn to the site by an enduring fascination with the threshold between sea and shore. My focus soon shifted, as I became increasingly intent upon the substance and movements of the ocean itself.

The preliminary exercise, to draw the course of a single wave from crest to break, initiated a struggle to find the media and marks that best suited the subject. Quick, gestured lines best capture the volume in motion, while tone forms a textured, rolling surface. The surface is sculpted to evoke the ocean's swell, the sense of bulging out from and collapsing into a void, and is carved to articulate crest and trough. The wave appears as a multifaceted event within a surface, with moments of activity balanced by areas of latency. The wave drawings, having shed any sense of place, are isolated frames of frozen motion or portraits. This realization sparked a drastic change in scale, which reveals the horizon.

The drawing of the ocean describes the threshold between sea and sky. The formidable horizon defines a limit, while the edges of the frame subside. A vacuous central gulf replaces the swell. The ocean is an impenetrable identity, an infinitely enigmatic chasm, and an inexhaustible subject to explore through drawing.

FIGURE 22

Conté crayon, pencil, and gesso on canvas

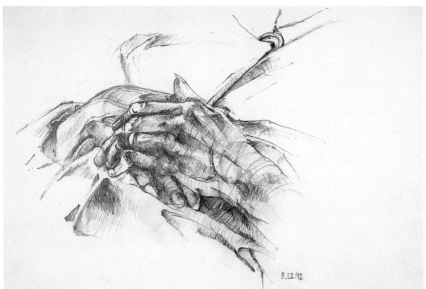

GRANDMOTHER STUDIES

ANIK PEARSON

My grandmother slept in her hospital bed, in what we knew to be her final days. My grandfather and I waited for her to wake up—we sat in her room for hours. We were at a loss for words. Realizing that it was a key moment in the history of the family, I wanted to record the circumstance, not leave it to memory alone. Photography seemed too graphic, naked, and morbid a medium to use in this case. Drawing was the only respectful way to capture the moment. It was a great relief to be doing something constructive during the vigil. Drawing enabled me to focus on something other than the event, on the landscape of her face and hands—each line in her face, the underlying structure of her bones, and the stretching and sagging of her skin between her knuckles and sinews. It was a way to explore the marks left in evidence of her long life and to honor her in that life.

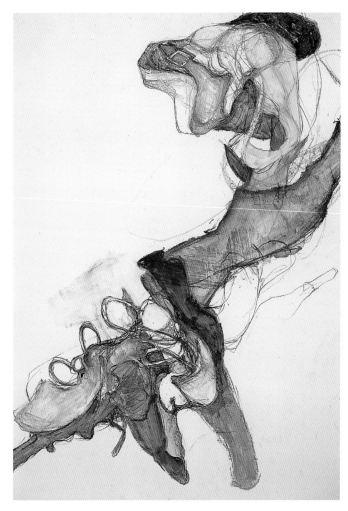

Oil bar, oil paint, and
charcoal pencil on paper

VOIDS, MATTER, SHADOWS

ALEXANDRA KISS

Architecture has given me an insatiable curiosity to explore and understand the sectional nature of inhabited space, and a desire to investigate the imprints our bodies leave in the spaces they occupy. This series of drawings began with frustrated attempts at seeing and drawing the space gathered and enclosed by old worn-out shoes that I had begun to collect. With the passing of time, shoes accumulate fundamental traces of our bodies—our weight imprints in their lining and soles, our way of walking deforms them in a unique manner, and the characteristic shapes of our feet press into them. These objects are portraits of their owners, lending an initially inanimate mass-produced object an animate existence. Sectioning the shoes was the method used to investigate and discover their inner space, to encounter the human trace. The shadows give them a trace of their own as the interstice between their matter, the external light, and their spatial context. The act of drawing articulates their distinct and separate existence, in the same way that the dweller impresses himself into the space he occupies and leaves behind a space that will be forever changed by what has come to pass through it.

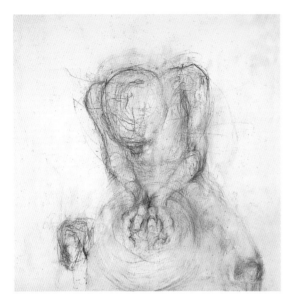
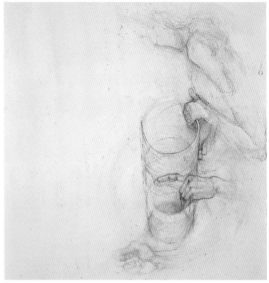

FIGURES **26** AND **27**

Oil paint, pencil, and
charcoal pencil on paper

CENTERING A POT

ANNE ROMME

On the fourth floor of The Cooper Union Foundation Building, I discovered a couple of neglected clay wheels and decided to use them as the basis of my advanced drawing project. Being a self-taught potter before studying architecture, I had always been fascinated by the process of creating space (a pot) through a controlled, fast-spinning mass. The only possible way of transforming the clay into a container is by holding the hands absolutely still about the center of the wheel while the clay rotates—otherwise centrifugal forces throw the clay off balance. The process is tactile: only when I close my eyes, concentrate, and feel can I judge if the clay is perfectly centered, if my hands use the right amount of force, and if the relationship between the thickness of the walls and the rotation speed is correct. To translate that into a drawing project was a challenge.

I used multiple semitransparent layers in an attempt to build up space in the drawing, hoping that it would echo the memory coded into my hands and body. Hard pencil enabled me to use multiple thin lines during my search for the form, working mostly from memory but also with the help of photographs. With layers of thin white oil paint in between, I could fix the pencil lines as an airy ghost for the next layer of drawing.

The most important lesson that I took with me from first-year drawing was that of understanding a piece of drawing paper as a site on which to create space. In the process of translating a spatial, temporal experience (of making a pot) into a series of drawings, I investigated how different strategies of composition could represent the relationships between the body and the space it inhabits in the different stages of transforming the mass of clay into space.

Dry pastel and wet brush
on paper

PORTRAIT
OF MY HUSBAND

FANI BUDIC

Of his best-known painting, *Arrangement in
Grey and Black* (1871), James Abbott McNeill
Whistler said, "To me it is interesting as a
picture of my mother; but what can or
ought the public care about the identity of
the portrait?" Likewise, my subjects were
people close to me and who were patient
enough to sit still for a while: my mother, my
friends, and Stephen, who later became my
husband.

As an architecture student, I used graphite ink and black and white photography as a
medium of constructing plans, sections, and
elevations. Color was not something I had
ever used to explore spatial relationships.
The Advanced Drawing seminar allowed me
to draw a series of portraits using dry pastels
and a wet brush that would turn portions of
the drawing into watercolor. I soon realized
that the arrangement of color is as much a
figure in its own right as any subject occupy-
ing space in a portrait.

*Arrangement in Blue and Yellow, Portrait of
my Husband* focuses not only on the stillness
of a person enveloped in reading but also
space defined by the motion of dark blue
and light yellow tones juxtaposed around
the figure.

PORTRAIT
OF MY WIFE

STEPHEN MULLINS

My subjects were always friends—those who were available and interested in posing for a few hours. In exchange I would pose for them. This mutual arrangement led me to develop a collection of drawings of (and by) the most important people in my life, including my wife, Fani.

In this drawing I investigated two spatial concepts: first the concept of enclosure and second the shared properties of space and body. Space wraps around the figure and around the book, chair, floor, and walls. Layers of enclosures nest one around another and create an effect of interiority. The area of the drawing was only a few feet; as a result my point of view was very close to the subject. The tight workspace encloses the viewer within the interiority of the drawing.

In the drawing space is treated in the same manner as flesh. The difference between the two occurs only through slight variations in their drawn qualities. The use of erasures, smudges, and lines distorts and extends the body. This creates an intervening of space, time, kinetics, and immersion.

FIGURE 29

Charcoal and red and black chalk on paper

FABRIC AND SKELETON

DASHA KHAPALOVA

The project originally began with an elevated subway bridge in Brooklyn that had developed a series of underbellies as the result of the stretching out of the mesh fabric that was installed underneath it to catch any falling debris. These volumes, hanging from the frame of the bridge, were transparent and torn in places so that you could see through the fabric and its various layers to the bridge beyond. The ideas of seeing through and seeing in, as well as layering and structure, were the central themes explored throughout the semester.

I studied the skeleton as an analogous structure to the bridge, first on its own and then with fabric draped over it in order to develop a language with which to explore the conditions common to both subjects. In the skull and the various openings that hint at what goes on inside, as well as the structural layering of the various bones and the careful relationships between the bones and voids, I found an inexhaustible subject. The culmination of the semester's study began with a chiffon-draped skeleton used to measure and record something almost imperceptible in relation to what shapes it (the skeleton, which also has its own condition of transparency). Through this struggle emerged a new level of understanding of the language that lies in the nuances of a line, which has greatly impacted my architectural thought.

ANGELS: THE ANATOMY OF WINGS

PIERRE GUETTIER

The drawings were completed during a period of my life in which the subject of angels unfolded into spatial possibilities. During a visit to Chartres I was struck by the carved angels embedded amongst the secular figures within the tympanum walls of the cathedral. In these carvings I saw relationships between the celestial and terrestrial figures materialize, as if one could not be complete without the other. This synergy led me to a drawn investigation of the celestial figure as a physical and spiritual presence. The premise was simple: construe and draw an angel—the elevated figure, the body in suspension—as the subject. The early drawings situated the angel in a space of gravitational tension, but the mobility of the subject proved difficult to animate without overdramatizing. As the drawings developed, guided by dialogues with Sue Gussow, my focus turned to animating the structure with the joints, the articulation of hinges, and the definition of the bones. The physiognomy of the angel drawings physicalized from this grounded structure. The singular figure in a suspended state of animation defines the occult nature of the subject.

FIGURE 31

Charcoal on paper

CAMERA OBSCURA

DAVID PETERSEN

FIGURE 32

Pastel and charcoal on
paper

This project documents the relationship between interior space and site as viewed from within a camera obscura moving from Bedford-Stuyvesant in Brooklyn to the Lower East Side of Manhattan. In order to reduce cost, I used old drafting tables made of solid pine to construct the walls and door of the camera. The completed camera stood seven feet two inches tall, five feet wide, and six feet five inches long, weighing over three hundred pounds. A simple pinhole lens with a diameter of 1/8 inch provided a dim, uniformly soft image with an infinite depth of field.

The camera projected the image upside down and backwards. I drew over the hazy projection, trying to find cohesive form in the play of shadows covering the interior wall. But the interior of the camera was too dark to produce a completed drawing. As I drew over the projection, the image became increasingly difficult to see and the interplay between its various parts was lost. I was unable to distinguish between static objects in the projection and the black charcoal lines on the page; this confusion on the page eventually forced me out of the camera to finish my drawings. As I worked on the drawings in the studio, the act of drawing took on greater force as I made the image resonate with my memory of the experience of occupation and perception inside the camera.

Over the course of this extended production, I knew that the project could end at any time, that I would eventually return to the last place I had left the camera and find it gone. The camera did finally disappear from the East River Park in late November. In the end, I had pushed the camera through seven miles of New York's streets over the course of ten weeks.

FIGURES **33** AND **34**

Charcoal pencil, ink wash, and gesso on paper (left); charcoal pencil on paper

CHESS HOUSE

CHRISTINA A. YESSIOS

The city inspires—ideas unfold from unexpected encounters and frame the projects. Capturing intimate and candid moments without influencing the subject's reaction to an intruder compelled and formed the basis for this project.

When I came upon the Chess House, it was apparent that my presence would go unnoticed—the players inside the transparent storefront were completely absorbed in the contest. I found a corner in this small room, usually packed with players and spectators in-between games, and entered their world through their facial expressions. The portraits of the chess players disclosed to me the openness of the space and the unconstrained demeanor of those involved, taken over by the game and its tactics. I became captivated by the tension of the competition and the possibility of creating relationships based solely on playing the game together.

After a number of sessions, after having become acquainted with the Chess House and the community within it, my perspective shifted away from the portrait. I found myself low on the floor looking up to the table, the horizon of the game and the chessboard. My focus and framing shifted to the table datum that had always subtly been part of the portrait drawings, defining part of the space without necessarily being present: how the body leaned against the table or a hand moved a pawn, then moved back to rest on a lap or the edge of the table.

The chessboard is a microcosm across which the hands of the players became detached from the rest of the body. The close-up, X-ray view of the chessboard led to more portrait drawings and further defined the player, his entire presence in relation to the chessboard and the opponent. In the final drawings I attempted to use everything I observed in prior studies to inform the overall space of the game.

THE GREETING

SONY DEVABHAKTUNI

I had seen Bill Viola's work *The Greeting* (1995) based on Jacopo Pontormo's painting of the same name, several years before I started at Cooper. The images from Viola's video stayed with me: two women are interrupted by a third, the action unfolding in slow motion so that each gesture and glance resonate, the stillness accumulating.

I had stills from *The Greeting* filed away and decided that they could be the subject of my Advanced Drawing project my final year at Cooper. I used three color images and began working with them individually. In fifteen-minute sketches using graphite pencil, I learned certain lines: the neck, heel, the curves of fabric, of the stomach. From there I worked in a larger format with multiple images at once. I worked for several minutes with each still, going back and forth so that a single drawing contained the three moments and also, perhaps, the time in-between.

Finally Sue Gussow suggested I work with color. I had used color since the short studies but only a timid and unsure mark here and there. Viola's film is remarkably vibrant, and I wanted to explore this aspect of the work. The results were a mess.

But for the first time in my drawing, I felt a kind of liberty—perhaps color introduced a sensibility removed from the architectonic considerations that had structured my thinking about drawing. I worked with oil sticks in dark tones, smearing the color on the canvas, fascinated by the way it slid over the surface. In time, I learned that I could *draw* with this new material, that I could use color to build structure.

I have not seen these drawings for several years; I remember being unsatisfied with the result. I felt like I had missed something: perhaps I should have worked from the video and not stills, started working with color sooner, or taken the work further from its figurative origins. It was difficult, this sense of having made strides but at once feeling doubt. I recognize now that this was Gussow's gift to me: to show me that place between uncertainty and epiphany that is the necessary site of creation.

FIGURE 35

Graphite and oil bar on paper (see also p. 131)

PORTRAIT
AS LANDSCAPE

CECILIA RODGERS

FIGURE **36**

Pen and ink wash on paper

The work in this project spans two years during which I focused on portraits of the same subject—my mother. I first drew the face as a landscape, zooming into the frame in order to focus in on one part, such as the eye. However, this erased the complexity and completeness of the facial expression, and details became less individualized. I widened the view in order to let in more of the face. Only then was I able to appreciate how the negative space of the face could flow through the drawing, like water running over the page.

These drawings are the largest I have ever made. They were completed in the bedroom of my apartment, which is quite small. I could only distance myself six feet from the drawing, and even then I was standing on my bed. It was a revelation to see them pinned up in the larger space of the studio.

SEPTEMBER 11, 2001

GERRI DAVIS

On my way to school the vacant streets echoed the muted sounds of radio newscasts. A man pointed toward the sky behind me—it was yellow and dark with smoke. Once at school our class relocated to the roof to witness the event unfolding. I took my sketchbook along. Drawing from the falling city was not a choice that I made but came more as an unavoidable, intuitive response to my desire to comprehend what was happening before me. For me, drawing is the most immediate way to understand the physical world. When events become so complicated that I am unable to wrap my mind around them, as in this case, drawing is the only way I can understand.

FIGURE 37

Compressed charcoal and whiteout on paper

TIMOTHY COLLINS

There are times when we are reminded of the very real presence of what we build. With the destruction of the World Trade towers, we came to face what our edifices might mean to us. The devastation wrought on lower Manhattan revealed the endemic conditions of fragility and mortality possessed by all cities.

Ineluctably present at that dreadful time, I was confronted by a disaster that completely overwhelmed my faculties. Immediately, I raced to obtain paper and drawing supplies from the local art store, returning to record the event that was unfolding in front of me. I could provide no other service but to document—to serve as a witness.

FIGURE 38 *above*

Vine and compressed charcoal, black pastel, gesso, watercolor pencil, red oil paint, and collage on paper

MERSIHA VELEDAR

I am a Bosnian New Yorker. This is the city where my family and I remade our home. On September 11, 2001, the very idea of home was again attacked. It is difficult to make what people call art out of an event so raw and personal. Drawing from the event was both my escape and my dialogue with the horror of it. The attack transformed New York into a groundless city—my drawings document that internal perception.

FIGURE 39 *right*

Watercolor and charcoal on paper

PART III

DRAWING IN PRACTICE
POSTGRADUATE WORK

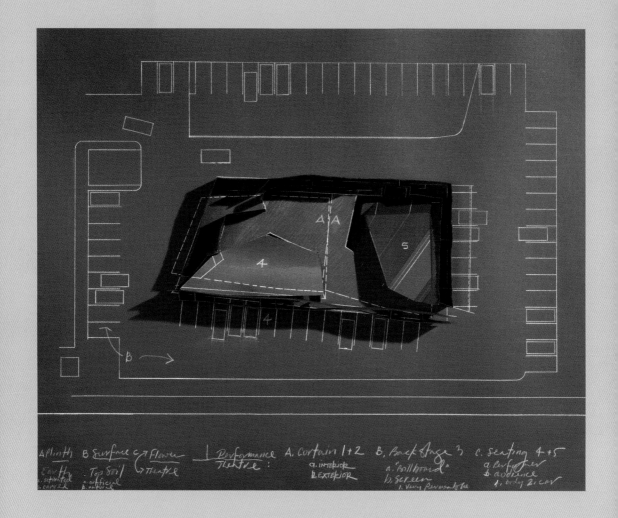

In the era before computer-generated graphics became the lingua franca of architectural practice, architects needed to be able to draw. They carried sketchbooks in which they noted ideas and kept travel journals for sketching buildings. The architect would think with drawing hand in motion. For some contemporary architects, the *premiere pensée* still comes from (or with) the hand roaming the paper.

Paul Henderson of Sigler Henderson Studio has, for over a decade, manufactured his own series of sketchbooks composed of 8½ × 11 copy sheets of drawings, letters, and other paper memorabilia, folded into quarters so that the older material is hidden in the interior, or occasionally revealed (figures 2–4). The backsides of these works provide surfaces for further use—new drawings and ideas for projects, images of his family, mementos, or random items of visual appeal are collaged on them. The books hold a constant conversation between the architect's personal and professional life.

In François de Menil's sketchbooks (figures 1, 5–7), he ponders details and structural elements and works out plans. In the pages concerning the Byzantine Fresco Chapel Museum (1997), a thoughtful study of a child's head appears (as if a child had just entered the room). The shape of the boy's beautifully rounded crown resonates with the chapel's dome.

Two architects' postgraduate investigations utilize drawing as a means to achieve a personal archeology, revisiting sites from their earlier lives, sites imbued with memory. In his Cappadocia landscape drawings, Firat Erdim revisits the wind-and-water-eroded landscape of his native Turkey. (Figures 8–9) The giant formations pictured in his drawings contain the history of Hittite temples and the remains of hidden cities and monasteries built by the first Christian colony founded by St. Paul. In drawing them Erdim mines his childhood landscape for visions that "have been coming back to me throughout and beyond my architectural education. Drawing has allowed me to explore a spatial unconscious."

In his Pittsburgh industrial landscape series, James Hicks likewise revisits a remembered landscape. (Figures 10–11) A portion of that landscape was the site of Hicks's thesis. In subsequent years he continued drawing from the site where his thesis project was located—unfolding the landscape as a map might show first one and then another portion of the region. His elegantly constructed drawings have the clarity of informed observation. Uninflected by atmospheric softening, the rocks, constructions, and trees are all of a cloth. Although the drawings display Hicks's mastery of Renaissance perspective, the entire folio opens out the Pittsburgh landscape like an axonometric projection.

Morris Sato Studio provides plan views in both the concept drawing and the photographic image of LightShowers installation. (Figures 12–13) The drawing is a fluid investigation of the interchange between the project's temporal and physical dimensions. While technical data will be plugged into later working documents, here Morris Sato explores the space created by light, water, sound, and human presence.

In the Fenquihi Station Bridge—Reiser + Umemoto's project in Taiwan to be completed in 2010—there is the imprint of each of their early and career-long preoccupations. The illustration for the bridge gives evidence of Reiser's immersion (since his student days) in drawings from the Renaissance. (Figure 14) Raphael is present in Reiser's use of fabric to link together the discreet forms of human bodies. The basket-weave geodetic structure of the bridge integrates Umemoto's fascination with weaving and fabric with Reiser's attraction to the connection of fabric to body. (Figures

15–16) Spanning across the rails, the bridge blooms from an uphill roof to fold downward and sit on a station roof below.

Peter Lynch developed a language of representation consistent with his personal philosophy: "Architecture, like alchemy, is a process of transmutation [in which] mixed and formless matter is changed to material of lasting value."[1] Lynch avails himself of one of the most humble (and unforgiving) means of representation and reproduction—the linoleum block. (Figure 17) In his spare use of lines cut singly, grouped together or curving where he wills them, Lynch describes edge, light, and even animation. In a linoleum-block print of North Quad, clouds roll past sunlit facades.

The several sketchbooks of Pablo Castro and Jennifer Lee reflect meditations on their project BEATFUSE!, OBRA Architects' PS1 installation, 2006, in which seven interconnected shells create a condition of interiority in an open space. (Figures 18–20) Much as in a plan drawing in which interior elements might acknowledge the exterior walls, these shells rise up and address the walls of existing buildings at the PS1 site. The plywood-and-mesh structures encompass pools, water misters, and light strainers, which continuously draw shapes in the mist.

As a Rome Prize scholar in 1994, Karen Bausman invented a mode of representation that reconfigures the conventions of architectural drawing practice. In her designs for Warner Brothers' Performance Theater (Los Angeles, California, 1999), she inscribes plan and section in one action on paper. (Figures 21–23) The sheet of paper is the site where the graphic and conceptual possibilities of the medium merge to forge a unique imprimatur.

In the work of these architects, the relationship between hand and mind is seamless. While several use drawing for representation and presentation (Bausman, Lynch, and Reiser + Umemoto), all use drawing as a means of expressing and clarifying their thought. For example, in the practice of Reiser + Umemoto drawing serves both generative and regenerative roles. OBRA's many sketchbooks explore myriad ideas in an array of drawing media—watercolor, pencil, pen and ink, and markers. François de Menil keeps a sketchbook with him constantly.

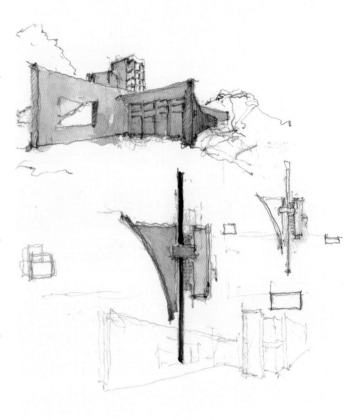

FIGURE 1

François de Menil, plan and study perspective of Foundation Watermill, an unrealized project, for theater director Robert Wilson, 1992. Pencil and watercolor on sketchbook paper.

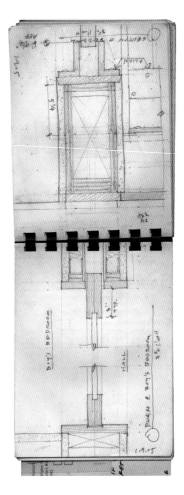

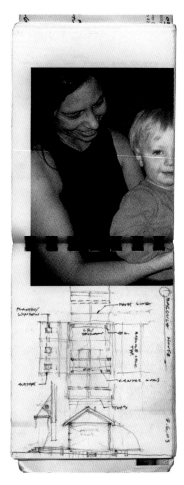

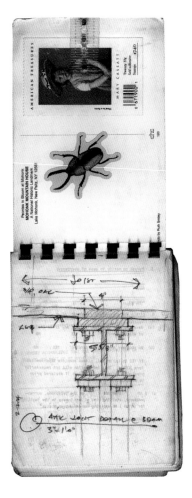

FIGURE 2

Paul Henderson, construction drawing sketches for pocket door assembly and details in the architect's home, 2005

FIGURE 3

Henderson, reproduction of a photograph of the architect's wife and son, adjacent to a study for a country house with bascule decks that close the house when not occupied, 2003

FIGURE 4

Henderson, sketch of an attic joist detail showing the reveal between the ceiling and the steel beam in the architect's home, adjacent to a bug sticker (a gift from the architect's sons) and a Cassatt sticker from the United States Postal Service, 2004

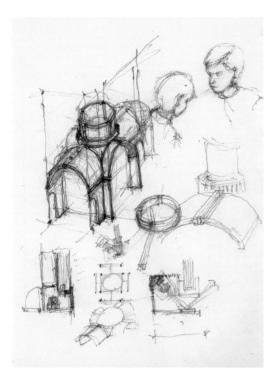

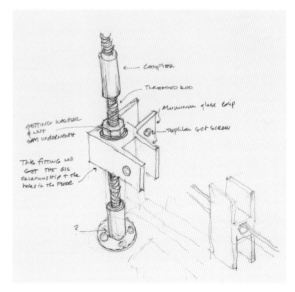

Firat Erdim, Cappadocia
drawings, 2002. Pencil on
paper.

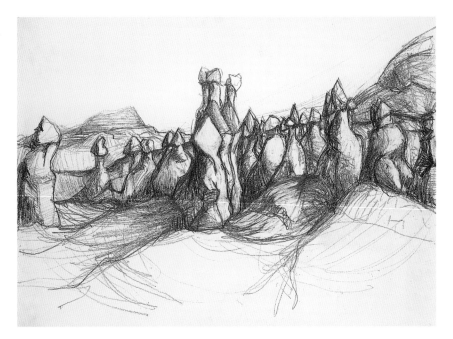

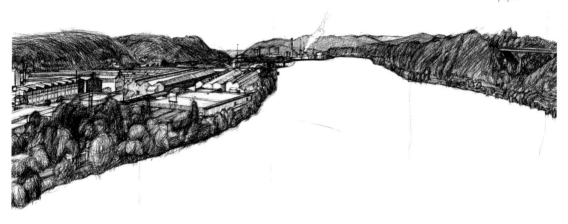

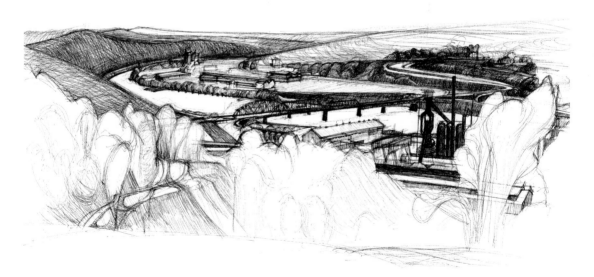

Yoshiko Sato and
Michael Morris, plan for
LightShowers installation,
Delaware Center for the
Contemporary Arts,
Wilmington, 2006.

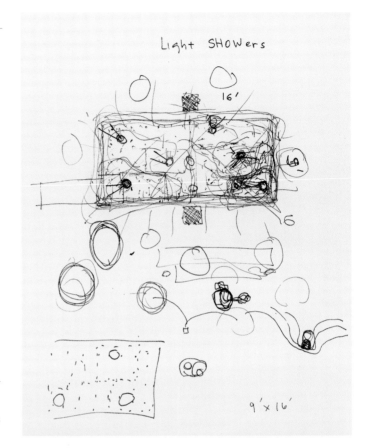

Morris Sato Studio,
photograph of plan view of
LightShowers. Video images
by Paul Ryan.

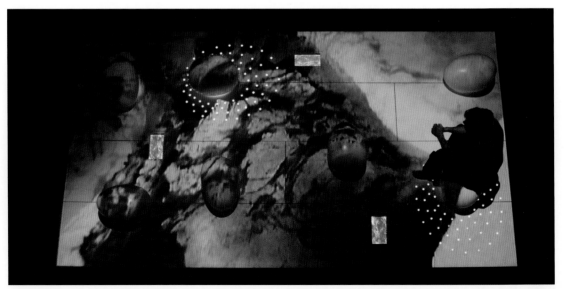

FIGURE 14 *left8*

Reiser + Umemoto, drawing of view of plaza at Fenchihu, Alishan Mountain, Taiwan, with Raphaelesque figure grouping, 2003. Pen and ink wash on paper.

FIGURE 15 *above*

Reiser + Umemoto, wood model of bridge at Fenchihu at ¼ scale. Shown at the American Pavilion, Venice Biennale, 2004.

FIGURE 16 *right*

Reiser + Umemoto, studies of Geodetic structure of bridge at Fenchihu, 2003. Colored pencil on paper.

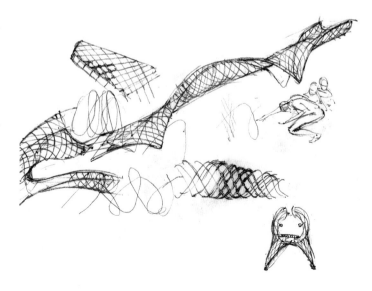

FIGURE 17 *above*

Peter Lynch, block print of
North Quad, a proposal
for a high school and community college in Bushwick,
Brooklyn, New York, 1992.
Linoleum block print on
rice paper.

FIGURE 18 *right*

Pablo Castro and
Jennifer Lee, sketch for
PS1 BEATFUSE! installa-
tion, 2005. Watercolor,
ink and pencil on
sketchbook paper.

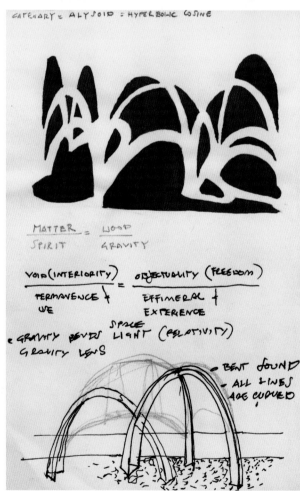

FIGURE 19 *above*

Castro and Lee, PS1
BEATFUSE! installation,
Long Island City, New York,
2006.

FIGURE 20 *left*

Castro and Lee, sketch for
PS1 BEATFUSE! installation,
2006. Pen and ink wash on
sketchbook paper.

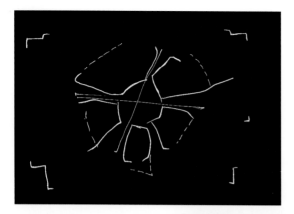

FIGURE 21 *left*

Karen Bausman, plan drawing of Warner Brothers' Performance Theater, Los Angeles, California, 1999. White pencil on black Fabriano paper.

FIGURE 22 *right*

Bausman, constructed drawing for Warner Brothers' Performance Theater. White and blue pencil on black Fabriano paper. (see also p. 161)

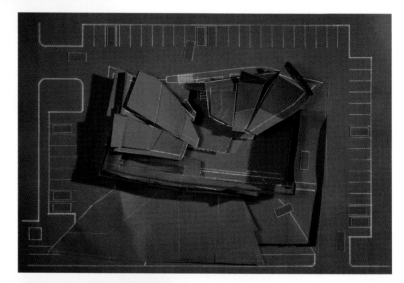

FIGURE 23 *left*

Bausman, supermodel of Warner Brothers' Performance Theater. Basswood and paper.

NOTES

INTRODUCTION

1. Johann Wolfgang von Goethe, *Elective Affinities*, trans. David Constantine (Oxford and New York: Oxford University Press, 1994), 120, 125, 127, 147, 155.
2. Paul Valéry, "Degas, Dance and Drawing," in *Degas, Manet, Monisot*, trans. David Paul, Bollingen Series, vol. 12 (New York: Pantheon Books, 1960), 36.
3. Ibid., 37.
4. Octavio Paz, "Chillida del Hierro al Reflejo," in *Sombras y Obras: Arte Y Literatura* (Barcelona: Seix Barral, 1983), 218. Translation by Dore Ashton.
5. Aristotle, *Aristotle's Poetics*, trans. S. H. Butcher (New York: Hill and Wang, 1961), 104.

WHERE IT ALL BEGINS: PEAS IN A POD

1. Berton Roueche, "The Talk of the Town," *New Yorker*, August 9, 1979, 23.

BELL PEPPERS, GARLIC, BROKEN SHELLS, STILL LIFES

1. K. G. Boon, *Rembrandt: The Complete Etchings* (New York: Harry N. Abrams, 1963), 217.
2. Jane Fearer Safer and Frances McLaughlin Gill, *Spirals from the Sea* (New York: C. N. Potter, 1982), 17–18.

HANDWRITING: THE SCRIBBLE PAGE

1. Saul Steinberg, *The Passport* (London: Hamish Hamilton, 1954).

LESSONS FROM THE MASTERS: HOMAGE AND REINVENTION

1. Frederick Hartt, *History of Italian Renaissance Art* (New York: H. N. Abrams, 1963), 515–16.
2. Patrick Nuttgens, *The Story of Architecture*, 2nd ed. (London: Phaidon, 1997), 182–87, 256–57.
3. Aurora Cuito and Cristina Montes, *Antoni Gaudí: Complete Works* (Berlin: Feirerabend, 2003), 51–52.

4. Judith A. Barter, ed., *Mary Cassatt: Modern Woman* (New York: H. N. Abrams, 1998), 72, 103.

THE DUMB OBJECT

1. Cited by Simon Schama, in "Rembrandt's Ghost," *New Yorker*, March 26, 2007, 40.

FLOWERS, PLANTS, AND MONDRIAN

1. Harry Holtzman and Martin James, eds., *The New Art, the New Life: The Collected Writings of Piet Mondrian* (Boston: G.K. Hall, 1986), 118.

TREES

1. Colin Tudge, *The Tree: A Natural History of What Trees Are, How They Live, and Why They Matter* (New York: Crown, 2006), 3.
2. Ibid., 75.

DIRTY DRAWING: ADVANCED PROJECTS

1. Friedrich Nietzsche, *The Birth of Tragedy*, trans. Walter Kaufmann (New York: Vintage Books, 1967). First published 1872.

DRAWING IN PRACTICE: POSTGRADUATE WORK

1. Peter Lynch, *The Cranbrook Monographs* (Bloomfield Hills, MI: Cranbrook Academy of Art & Telos Art Publications, 2003), 12.

GLOSSARY

Aerial Perspective An illusion of distance achieved by modifying the contrast of the tonal values of both shapes and lines as objects recede from the observer.

Blind Contour This method involves the eye slowly following any line at the edge or on the surface of the object being studied, without looking down at the paper, as the hand and pencil (or pen) slowly record the eye's observation. In this pedagogy occasional glances at the paper are allowed. At such moments the hand should cease to draw.

Cast Shadow The shape of the tone an object throws onto an adjoining object or plane as it intercepts a source of light, distinct from the tone employed to render the shadow side of an object.

Cross-hatching This method involves overlapping a set of hatch marks with another group of hatched lines, drawn at an opposing angle and resulting in small diamonds or squares.

Foreshortening The contraction of the shapes of body forms or other objects as they recede from the observer to create the illusion of projection or depth. Key to the process is keen observation of the unexpected shapes—both positive and negative—that occur in foreshortened positions.

Freestyle Drawing The term "freestyle" drawing signifies the student's complete authority over material, size, or manner of drawing—that aspect commonly referred to as "style." In some assignments certain aspects of freestyle are curtailed in accord with the demands of the problem.

Gesture How the major masses of the body—head, chest, pelvis—are rotated around the central axis of the spine, combined with the posture of the limbs. By metaphoric extension, a major movement or thrust in a drawing may be termed the drawing's gesture or spine.

Hatching A group of closely spaced parallel lines—usually on the diagonal—that are grouped together to create a tonal shape.

Local Color The surface color of an object, without influence from either shadow or highlight. Local color may be altered or ignored, as desired, to enhance the design of the drawing.

Negative Space When a form is drawn, the leftover space between the shapes is negative space. It is an essential concept in drawing and design—helpful in measuring distance between one form and another—and an invaluable tool in composition.

Passageway A strategy for leading the viewer's eye through the drawing, by means of contiguous darker shapes or lines that continue from one object to another.

Scribble Drawing Creating markings that are mimetic of the movement of the hand in script writing but without clear letters or words.

Skeletal Articulation The configuration of two or more bones at a joint, which enable the motion of the skeleton. Practice in drawing skeletal articulation is key to drawing other articulations—tree limbs and branches, joinery in furniture, framing, etc.

Spatial Ambiguity A concept employed to engage and tease the eye. In spatial ambiguity, objects may appear to be spaces and spaces assume volume. By employing shared contour lines and tonal values between close and distant shapes, forms laying in different planes may appear to be next to one another.

Subtlety and **Vagueness** Subtle is derived from the French term *soutil*, meaning "finely woven." The word connotes acute observation, understatement, and softness. The novice artist often confuses subtlety with vagueness—indecisive shapes, confused edges, randomness of intention. Subtlety is desirable, vagueness never is.

Tone and **Tonal Areas** Tone appears in a range of gray values graded between white and black and creates shapes. Such shapes, or tonal areas, can greatly influence the graphic readability of a work.

Underdrawing A light, rapid study in which the artist marks the major masses of the figure or object under consideration. Subsequent marks further define the artist's gathering intention.

Visual Surprise The thing you did not expect to see—that element that initially catches your eye or arises from an epiphany during the drawing process. In its essence it is discovery.

CONTRIBUTORS

John Alber
101 fig. 2; 118 fig. 10 (1997–98)

Michal Attia
121 fig. 2 (2001–2)

Asa Barak
114 fig. 4 (2001–2)

Karen Bausman
161; 171 figs. 21, 22, 23 (1999)

Jody Bell
117 fig. 8 (1998–99)

Jiri Boudnik
37 fig. 3 (1993–94)

Masha Braslavsky
58 fig. 6 (1985–86)

Lorna Bravo
37 fig. 2; 61 fig. 5; 85 fig. 6
(1994–95)

Fani Budic
150 fig. 28 (1994)

Robert Carter
27 fig. 11; 107 fig. 14 (1981–82)

Pablo Castro and Jennifer Lee
170 fig. 18 (2005)
171 figs. 19, 20 (2006)

Lis Cena
140 figs. 12, 13 (2006)

Amber Chapin
57 fig. 5; 116 fig. 7 (1999–2000)
138 fig. 10 (2001)

Michael Chen
90 fig. 5 (1992–93)

Aka Chikasawa
25 fig. 8 (1990–91)

Netta Cocos
119 fig. 13 (1999–2000)

Robert Cohen
54 fig. 5; 60 fig. 2 (1979–80)

Timothy Collins
159 fig. 38 (2001)

Christina Condak
33 fig. 5; 75 figs. 8, 9 (1989–90)

Dale Corvino
52 fig. 2 (1982–83)

Michael Cullum
73 fig. 5 (1983–84)

Paul Dallas
141 fig. 14 (2006)

Gerri Davis
50 fig. 10; 68 fig. 4; 84 fig. 5; 97
fig. 7; 117 fig. 9 (1999–2000)
158 fig. 37 (2001)

François de Menil
17 figs. 1, 2; 18 fig. 3; 23 fig. 4
(1982–83)
163 fig. 1 (1992)
165 figs. 5, 6 (1993)
165 fig. 7 (1997)

Sony Devabhaktuni
109 fig. 19 (1999–2000)
131; 156 fig. 35 (2002)

Christian Dickson
119 fig. 14 (1987–88)

Michael Dub
112 fig. 1 (2000–2001)

Wilton Duckworth
25 fig. 7; 63 fig. 2 (1981–82)

Gaustas Eigirdas
41 fig. 3 (2002–3)

Martin Eisler
95 fig. 3 (1996–97)

Firat Erdim
166 figs. 8, 9 (2002)

Grigori Fateyev
116 fig. 6 (1993–94)

Sue Ferguson Gussow
22 fig. 3 (2007)

Vicente Fernandez
103 fig. 7 (1984–85)

Arneá Ferrari
71 fig. 2; 107 fig. 15; 111 figs. 21, 22
(1994–95)

Natalie Fizer
24 fig. 6; 91 fig. 6; 122 fig. 3
(1984–85)

Emma Fuller
39 fig. 6 (2001–2)

Cheri Gandy
60 fig. 4 (1991–92)

Alexander Garcia
15; 28 fig. 12 (1993–94)

Jane Garvie
74 fig. 7; 80 fig. 5 (1994–95)

Christopher Geissler
43 fig. 1; 60 fig. 3; 67 fig. 2; 95
fig. 4; 101 figs. 3, 4 (1991–92)

Daniel Gil
109 fig. 18; 118 fig. 11 (2002–3)

Pierre Guettier
153 fig. 31 (1992)

Cagla Hadimioglu
54 fig. 6; 126 fig. 7 (1991–92)

Rebecca Haskins
83 figs. 2, 3; 84 fig. 4 (1994–95)

Paul Henderson
164 fig. 2 (2005)
164 fig. 3 (2003)
164 fig. 4 (2004)

James Hicks
26 fig. 9 (1986–87)
167 fig. 10 (1997)
167 fig. 11 (1999)

Steven Hillyer
69 fig. 6; 124 fig. 4 (1985–86)

Han-Hsi Ho
127 fig. 8 (1999–2000)

Michael Hodge
32 fig. 3 (1999–2000)

Nina Hofer
128 fig. 9 (1984–85)
134 figs. 3, 4 (1987)

Yeon Wha Hong
33 fig. 6; 39 fig. 5 (2000–1)
135 fig. 5 (2004)

Jeffrey Hou
89 fig. 3 (1985–86)

Angie Hunsaker
85 fig. 7 (1997–98)

John Kashiwabara
22 fig. 2 (1982–83)

Dasha Khapalova
152 fig. 30 (2006)

Frank Kiernan
42 fig. 5 (1990–91)

Alexandra Kiss
108 fig. 17 (2000–2001)
148 fig. 25 (2002)

Stan Krebushevski
100 fig. 1 (1981–82)

Charles Krekelberg
66 fig. 1; 73 fig. 4; 92 fig. 1; 98
    fig. 8; 119 fig. 15 (1992–93)

Szymon Kuczynski
105 fig. 10 (2000–2001)

Chi-Hsiu Lee
49 fig. 8 (1994–95)

Aaron Lim
106 figs. 11, 12 (2002–3)

Carlos Little
34 fig. 7 (1993–94)

Sharon Lobo
27 fig. 10; 70 fig. 1 (1986–87)

Aimee Lopez
41 fig. 2 (1992–93)

Julian Louie
42 fig. 4; 68 fig. 3; 106 fig. 13
    (2002–3)

Peter Lynch
170 fig. 17 (1992)

Gia Mainiero
139 fig. 11 (2005)

Dean Maltz
59 fig. 1; 94 fig. 2 (1979–80)

Salvatore Marrese
78 figs. 2–3; 104 fig. 8 (1981–82)

Maya Mawell
136 figs. 6–7 (2004)

Jane McAllister
81 fig. 1 (1987–88)

Daniel Meridor
64 fig. 3 (2002–3)
137 figs. 8–9 (2005)

Beth Miller
146 fig. 22 (2005)

Tirso Molina
40 fig. 1; 61 fig. 6; 64 fig. 4
    (1994–95)

Marguerite Montecinos
57 fig. 4 (1990–91)

Pia Moos
20 fig. 1 (1993–94)

Michael Morris and Yoshiko Sato
168 figs. 12, 13 (2006)

Stephen Mullins
51 fig. 1 (1990–91)
55 fig. 1 (2004)
151 fig. 29 (1993)

James Naughton
91 fig. 7 (1977–78)

Jose Ortez
144 figs. 18, 19 (2005)

Jesung Park
13 (2002–3)

Anik Pearson
58 fig. 7, 88 fig. 2 (1990–91)
147 figs. 23, 24 (1992)

David Petersen
154 fig. 32 (2006)

Gina Pollara
56 fig. 3 (1985–86)

Piotr Redlinski
87 fig. 1 (1996–97)

Jesse Reiser and Nanako
    Umemoto
169 figs. 14 (2003)
169 figs. 15 (2004)
169 fig. 16 (2003)

Cecilia Rodgers
157 fig. 36 (2005)

William Rohde
45 fig. 4 (1996–97)

Anne Romme
38 fig. 4; 110 fig. 20 (2001–2)
149 figs. 26, 27 (2003)

Taku Shimizu
48 fig. 7; 49 fig. 9; 99 fig. 9
    (1992–93)
132 fig. 1; 133 fig. 2 (1993)

Waicheong Shiu
108 fig. 16 (1994–95)

Saija Singer
99 fig. 10 (1992–93)

Martha Skinner
120 fig. 1 (1992–93)

Nellie King Solomon
96 fig. 6; 124 fig. 5 (1990–91)

Kee Hiang Song
14; 104 fig. 9 (1989–90)

John Soraci
8 (1981–82)

Tao Sule
102 fig. 5; 114 fig. 3 (1997–98)

Gerard Sullivan
113 fig. 2 (1984–85)

Nagi Suzuki
44 fig. 3 (1991–92)

Victoria Tentler
53 fig. 3; 114 fig. 5 (1992–93)

Anthony Titus
29 fig. 13 (1993–94)

Thomas Tsang
32 fig. 4; 56 fig. 2 (1994–95)

Nanako Umemoto
74 fig. 6 (1980–81)

Unknown Authors
23 fig. 5; 44 fig. 2; 69 fig. 5

Lars Van Es
65 fig. 5 (1997–98)

Mersiha Veledar
159 fig. 39 (2001)

Natalya Vidokle
46 fig. 5; 47 fig. 6 (1991–92)

Dieter Vischer
102 fig. 6 (2002–3)

Moeno Wakamatsu
31 fig. 2; 76 fig. 1; 80 fig. 6
    (1994–95)

Greta Waller
62 fig. 1; 119 fig. 12; 125 fig. 6
    (2002–3)

Richard Warden
129 fig. 10 (1983–84)

Adrienne Watson Campbell
53 fig. 4 (1990–91)

Daniel Webre
50 fig. 11 (2001–2)
145 figs. 20, 21 (2003)

David Weiland
142 figs. 15, 16 (2005)

Maria Westerstahl
30 fig. 1 (1995)
35 fig. 1; 65 fig. 6 (1994–95)

Nathaniel Worden
96 fig. 5 (1990–91)

Christina Yessios
155 figs. 33, 34 (2005)

Victoria Zaretsky
72 fig. 3 (1994–95)

Tamar Zinguer
79 fig. 4; 90 fig. 4 (1983–84)

Lauren Zucker
143 fig. 17 (2003)